GANGSTERS AND COPS

Prohibition, Corruption, and LAPD's Scandalous Coming of Age

James Bultema

ALSO BY JAMES BULTEMA

Non-Fiction

Guardians of Angels
A History of the Los Angeles Police Department 1869 – 2019

Unsolved Cold-Case Homicides of Law Enforcement Officers

The Protectors
A Photographic History of Police Departments in the United States

Fiction
Sea of Red (Fall 2023)

Documentary
Behind the Badge: An Insiders History of the Los Angeles Police Department

P.D. Publishing
7904 E. Chaparral Rd. PMB 239, #110
Scottsdale, AZ 85250

Website: https://www.jamesbultema.com/

This book was edited by Janice Obuchowski,
threepennyeditor.com

Cover design by Olivia M. Hammerman, ochbookdesign.com

Title photograph: Author's collection

Author photo by Carole Bultema

ISBN: 978-0-9974251-8-5   Hardcover
        978-0-9974251-6-1   Softcover

To my wife, Carole. My best friend for fifty-one years

Contents

Chapter 1

The Formative Years

* "Personally, I have no reluctance at leaving the force; the work is not pleasant. I will probably go to work next week in my blacksmith shop."

—Henry King, Chief of Police

* Note: All quotes in the book are presented as originally written, with no corrections or editing.

They stood around an old blackboard in the roll-call room of police headquarters. Some were still dressed in their duty uniforms, while other off-duty patrolmen had rushed to police headquarters. They were there to determine if they still had jobs. It was 1889, the day after New Year's. Small groups of men gathered in the room's corners, whispering about their chances of pinning on their Los Angeles Police badges for the next shift or turning them into the chief.

They were an odd lot of officers. Several had been on the force before and had been let go even though they had clean records. Still, others had been fired previously for "cause." Others had resigned, while many had been appointed for work they had completed during the most recent political campaign. In the nineteenth-century LAPD, your political party was more important for job security than how well you performed as a patrolman.

At midnight, a sergeant casually walked toward the blackboard carrying the future of those waiting. The officers parted as if that gesture might save their jobs. The "annual shake" notice the sergeant was about to post would have a simple notation next to each man's name. Either you were "on" or "off."

Thirty men rushed to the blackboard as the sergeant left to learn their fate. While several hooted joyfully, others hung their heads and walked from the room, wondering how they would break the news to their loved ones. Sadly, for Los Angeles Police Department members during this era, there was no job security. Politicians ran the police force, and everyone from the chief down had to play the game. Besides, four hundred other men waited in the wings to replace those who had just been let go.

A new city charter established a formal police commission to oversee the department. The commission-controlled appointments, dismissals, and promotions. It also set the general policy. The police commission was appointed by the Common City Council and was composed of four civilians: two Democrats and two Republicans. The mayor was also on the board but could not serve as chairman. The intent was to neutralize politics within the Los Angeles Police Department by politically dividing and balancing the police commission.

But many officials felt it was apparent that putting five politically motivated men in the same room would not make a depoliticized police force. Case in point: during the city elections of 1889, the mayor and city council were elected by an overwhelming Republican majority. The police commission interpreted that as a mandate to respond to the people's vote. Therefore, it was resolved that the force had to be composed of at least seventy-five percent Republicans for the next two years. As a result, more notices appeared on the blackboard.

Patrolman H. C. Garlock, a veteran of the Civil War, would have none of it. He had a *Los Angeles Times* reporter follow him as he went to the police commissioner to see why he, a Republican all his life, had been fired. He asked Police Commissioner D. Gilbert Dexter why he had been let go. "Well, I'm not sure what the specific charges were, but Commissioner Hervey Lindley has all the paperwork, so you ask him." As Garlock met with Lindley, the commissioner looked through the documentation and found Garlock's name. "You've been removed because you're being charged as a Democrat, and you did not vote in the last election." Garlock, a wily Civil War veteran, pleaded that he had always been a Republican. Lindley referred Garlock to police headquarters because that's where the report came from. Garlock then spoke to James Burns, the new chief, who said, "I told all the sergeants to make inquiries into each man" to see his political affiliation. When Garlock finally tracked down the sergeant, the officers said his only charge was that the officer had not voted. Like many other good men, Garlock was finished as an LA cop.

Politics' overpowering intrusion into the administration of the LAPD would continue for generations. One-hundred years later, Chief Willie Williams (1992– 1997) said politics was still a significant problem:

> Politics has greatly intruded into the day- to-day management activities of the Los Angeles Police Department; I don't think it takes a brain surgeon to see that...The chief in Los Angeles, I found out, is a very political person, whether you like it or not. I have twenty-one bosses: fifteen in council, one in the mayor's office and five in the commission...And I think, unfortunately, it is going to occur not just for me, but for those people who follow me, unless the public stands up and says, 'Media back off, politicians back off.' Let

this and all future chiefs of the LAPD do
their job but be accountable to the public
not the media.

It did not start that way. Politics wasn't an issue in the
middle of the nineteenth century for the little village of 1,600
souls of primarily Spanish and Mexican heritage. They went
about their business of farming, ranching, and trading,
essentially unbothered by the outside world. The padres
from the church enforced the existing laws. Content with
their lives but looking to the future, early community leaders
opted to become a city on April 4, 1850, just a few months
before California became the thirty-first state. The
municipality was christened The Town of Our Lady, the
Queen of Angels. Los Angeles began its march into
greatness.

In 1848, peace and tranquility in the Queen of Angels
changed forever with the discovery of gold in Sutter's Mill.
Soon 300,000 prospectors arrived with visions of getting
rich quickly. Mixed in were murderers, horse thieves,
gamblers, prostitutes, rowdy cowboys, displaced Indians,
cattle thieves, and outlaw gangs. Many came to Los Angeles
to escape the vigilante committees of San Francisco and the
mining towns of the north.

Lacking a law enforcement infrastructure to round up
these undesirables, the fledgling city soon became the

definition of the Wild West. More people were killed in LA in one week than in Tombstone, Arizona, in a decade. So-called law-abiding residents reacted with equal savagery. Lynch mobs soon formed, led on one occasion by the mayor of Los Angeles. Seeing bodies hanging from trees and ranch posts was not unusual as citizens went about their lives.

Death by violence was so common in Los Angeles that the crimes seldom received more than a few lines in the newspapers. For example: "Jose, a Mexican, was found shot to death in the Calle de los Negros area. An inquest found he died by violence from unknown persons." End of story, end of another life by violence.

The only courtroom many of these murderers would enter was some makeshift room where the vigilantes would hold court. Although San Francisco was reputed to be the vigilante capital of California, it had nothing on LA. In 1871, San Francisco executed eight criminals, but in Los Angeles, there were forty legal hangings and thirty-eight lynchings. And this figure did not include the twenty shot and lynched during the Chinese Massacre.

Years later, an eyewitness described how one vigilante committee operated in Los Angeles:

> I believe it was about the fourth day after my arrival that the prisoners, who had

been undergoing examination before the sub-committee, were brought to the Court House, where the final report of the committee was to be submitted to the great self-constituted court of justice-loving Americans.

Abbott's bath house was then used as a court house, and a high old court it was, too, I assure you. The place was packed to suffocation, with a dense crowd outside. Old Horse-Face presided over the court. The report of the committee was first read on the case...and the President then in a solemn voice said: "Gentlemen, the court is now ready to hear any motion." Whereupon a ferocious looking gambler mounted a bench and said: "I move that Reyes Feliz be taken to the hill and hung by the neck until he be dead."

"All in favor of the motion will signify the same by saying Aye!" said the president gravely. "Aye! Aye! Aye!" yelled the mob, and Reyes Feliz was a doomed man...All of this occurred on a Saturday, and the following day was set for carrying out into execution the sentence of the court. By the time the town was astir next morning the ugly gallows could be seen on Fort Hill, with its horrid arms extended, as though defying the vengeance of man, or invoking the God of Justice. At 9 o'clock a herald paraded the streets, ringing a large dinner bell, and with a loud voice summoning the faithful to the feast; When all was ready, the victims were given permission to speak. All maintained a dogged silence except the poor cobbler Sandoval [another person convicted], who made a brief speech. He hoped the great God would pardon his murderers as he pardoned them, and said that he died innocent, without a crime. They all kissed the crucifix, the rope was cut, the trap fell, and the five men were launched into eternity.

The few charged with keeping the peace in Los Angeles encountered extreme danger. Mexican desperadoes would ride into the city on night raids, and their first order of business was to brush aside the law. Using a reata which was a tightly woven hide or hair rope, two raiders would ride by an officer while swinging their reatas and strike the officer with such force that the lawman found himself lying on the dirt street, knocked out. With the peacekeepers out of the way, the crooks would conduct their raids and disappear into the night with their saddlebags full of loot.

Combined with urban growth, crimes such as these convinced the Common Council to establish a police force. By 1869, the city had grown fivefold to 5,700 residents. With wide-open vice and conditions that shaped Los Angeles into a mecca for criminal activity, the Common Council needed to act. It did so in late 1868. "On motion, resolved, that his Honor the Mayor appoint a City Police by and with the approval of the council to consist of four persons." Mayor Cristobal Aguilar, who spoke very little English, appointed four men (who quickly became six) on January 4, 1869. The city could not afford to pay these officers a salary, so they were paid a commission from the collection of fees, which included serving writs, returning lost or stolen property, and arresting fugitives.

Los Angeles Police was off to a rocky start. The first police department was led by William C. Warren, who split duties as city marshal and chief of police. Warren had a knack for law enforcement. He had been the town marshal for the previous decade and a deputy marshal for several years before that. A hard-headed farmer from Michigan, Warren, was killed by one of his officers, Joseph Dye, in an argument over the reward money for a Chinese prostitute. With guns blazing in the middle of Main and Temple (next to where City Hall is today), Dye killed the chief and subsequently won his battle in court when he was found not guilty on the grounds of self-defense.

The Common Council's failure to pay for a salaried police force contributed to what became known as the Chinese Massacre. The fee system encouraged corrupt practices. An officer might be given several warrants for a single location, such as a boarding house, but would make several trips with each document to collect multiple payments. As with Chief Warren, arguments were common, and the payment of fees pitted law enforcement officers against one another. One could get very desperate to put food on the table.

Many of the officers' duties did not include getting paid a commission and consequently received little attention from the politicians and the police. One deadly example was the lack of protection for arrestees and citizens from the ever-present lynch mobs. In 1871, a large, predominantly white mob murdered nineteen innocent Chinese residents. The police force's failure to stop the riot became one of the darkest days in Los Angeles law enforcement history. Several officers were even accused of taking part in the hangings. In response, the Common Council moved to establish a salaried police department and drop the fee system.

Five years after the Chinese Massacre, in 1876, the council established the Office of Chief of Police and ended the marshal position and the commissioned-based fee system. The Los Angeles Police Department had its first paid chief in German-born Jacob Gerkens, and a salaried thirteen-man police force. Gerkens had crossed the plains to

California in an ox cart. He was employed in teaming and freighting for one year and ran a ferry boat business in Yuma, Arizona. He then went from the sheep business to the grocery business and finally to the Los Angeles City Council.

Despite having no formal schooling, the ambitious thirty-four-year-old designed an attractive uniform, primarily so his officers would project a professional image. All men were required to wear a Western hat with a blue hip-serge coat. To complete the uniform, Gerkens oversaw the development of a striking eight-point silver star in the shape of a sunburst today called the Series One badge.

After serving as chief of the LAPD for one year, Gerkens took the position of assistant chief. From this point, police chiefs came and went in baffling succession. With few exceptions, the chiefs of the LAPD did not last long. From 1876 to 1889, thirteen years, sixteen men came and went through the office of the chief of police. This pattern would characterize the LAPD for generations to come.

By the close of the nineteenth century, big-city municipal police departments were being taken over by political machines, usually led by one powerful boss that commanded enough votes to maintain control of the city. Local police officers became pawns. Their assignments while walking their beats might include roughing up political opponents while keeping an eye on the politician-owned gambling halls, prostitution houses, and other assorted vice activities.

Officials in LA made changes at the top to fit their agendas. It was the spoils system working as designed. Policymakers awarded municipal jobs to loyal supporters, and retention depended upon continued service to the donor rather than the public. In 1889, Mayor John Bryson appointed all six of his sons to the police department.

Routinely, officers were transferred, fired, promoted, or dismissed at the direction of local politicians. If a patrolman wanted to keep his job, he did as ordered by the political machine rather than the police department.

Without the strong leadership of a chief of police, with no civil-service protection and thus no job security, the chief worried more about retaining his job than police corruption in the streets. Filling the void were the politicians who dispensed discipline that favored their schemes. Topping the list was the district councilman who controlled the patrolmen's beat. Either the patrolman did as the civilian told him, or he would be fired for trumped-up charges.

Consequently, less ethical patrolmen seized on illegal opportunities, and corruption took a foothold in the department. While some men made a career in the LAPD and did as they were ordered from within, many more assented to the politicians and enriched themselves at every opportunity. These dishonest police officers used the powers of arrest to make a quick buck. Looking the other way was more rewarding than simply collecting a meager paycheck. The most ruthless applied diligently to local politics, which earned them promotions and privileges. Accordingly, very few capable, honest men accepted the small salary and the low social standing that accompanied pinning on an LAPD badge.

Over the decades, the population in Los Angeles has risen as fast as a bamboo shoot in the jungle. From a population of 1,600 in 1850, LA grew to over 50,000 by 1890. Keeping pace with this expanded growth was prostitution and vice: there were houses of ill fame, bars, and casinos; there were pickpockets and con men; and there was an assortment of other predators who fed off the population.

Many patrolmen joined in this vice and political corruption. Many took payoffs that allowed illegal drinking, prostitution, and gambling on their beats. Thieves and pickpockets could apply their craft while the officer walked the other way, his pockets stuffed with cash.

Chiefs of police have not been exempt from

allegations of corruption. Henry King (1878–1880 and 1881–1883), who served for four years (during two different terms), is an example. King was born in Ireland in 1832 and raised in St. Louis. When he was twenty-two, he headed for California to seek his fortune in the gold fields. Later he moved to Los Angeles, becoming one of its earliest settlers. Until he became chief of police, King had run a successful business as a blacksmith.

In 1882, the fledgling *Los Angeles Times* ran a series of articles as the city council charged King with protecting vice. A pattern of police-protected vice emerged through the testimony of witnesses with firsthand knowledge of the events.

A prominent Los Angeles lawyer, H.T. Gage, testified about a "house of ill fame" and produced a diagram of the home where opium use, and prostitution occurred. Seeking the assistance of the LAPD, Mr. Gage went to police headquarters and walked into a room where several officers were sitting around talking. He showed Captain Thomas Cuddy, who was second in command and would be appointed the next chief of police, the map. After a casual look, Cuddy took his men and started "walking away indifferently." Gage was left alone and given no assistance from the LAPD.

At a subsequent criminal trial of several defendants from the house in question, Chief King was present and spent considerable time consulting with the defense when several witnesses for the prosecution did not appear. As it turned out, they had been arrested on false charges.

Five patrolmen testified to the sordid reputation of the house on Arcadia Street; their testimony detailed illegal acts associated with the charges. Later, two other officers stated Chief King ordered them to stay away from Chinatown, "We left it alone," When King was shown the diagram, he refused to discuss it.

Patrolman Jon Shafer, who had served under King, testified, "I was told by the chief [King] I had no business in Chinatown." Shafer said he had been bribed by one of the defendants, Ah Toy, to stay away from the house on Arcadia Street.

In February of 1882, the city attorney, J.T. Hazard, formally charged Chief King with dereliction of duty. In the charge, the future mayor of Los Angeles documented how the police department (consisting of just twelve men) failed to enforce any laws against the houses of prostitution, gambling establishments, and opium dens. With no cooperation from the police, Mr. Hazard hired a "special detective," who King refused to cooperate with. Hazard said,

"That since that time, the said chief of police [King] has in every means in his power endeavored to frustrate everyone…that this city attorney cannot convince anyone to assist and the police department will not cooperate." Frustrated, Hazard said, "A conviction of any Chinaman for any of the crimes is next to impossible."

With city officials coming after him, Chief King resigned and told a *Times* reporter, "Personally, I have no reluctance at leaving the force; the work is not pleasant. I will probably go to work next week in my blacksmith shop." The following week a passerby saw the former chief of police bent over his forge, making horseshoes.

While King went on pounding horseshoes, the nation was introduced to a reform movement that would have a lasting impact on the Los Angeles Police Department. It was called Progressivism, a movement of intense social and political reform. There would be times when the politicians ran with their collective tails between their legs while being chased by the reformers and times when they ruled the city with an iron fist and the reformers were on the defensive. The reformer delivering the first blow was a man who would go down in history as one of the most notable chiefs ever to wear an LAPD badge—John M. Glass.

Chapter 2

The Fight for Control of the

LAPD

"A political policeman is an unmitigated nuisance; the worst and most dangerous type of demagogue."

—John M. Glass, Chief of Police

Her name was Miss Adolphine Babut. She was a diminutive seventeen-year-old described as having the "sensual prettiness of rosy skin and full form." If not for an article in the *Los Angeles Times* in 1903, Babut would have been overlooked by history, with little of her existence ever known.

Babut came to represent everything wrong with Los Angeles in the awakening years of the twentieth century. The young girl was forced into prostitution by some of the vilest criminals in humanity.

Babut worked at her sister's art store in Paris, France, decorating pillows and leather goods for sixty cents a day. She was happy, and she was naïve. Minding the store by herself one day, she was approached by a couple pretending to be wealthy entrepreneurs. They dangled images of her moving to the United States, where she could make between one to three dollars a day working in their print shop with other French girls. After hearing tales of girls her age living joyously in America, she packed her scant belongings and snuck out of her sister's home to pursue her childish dreams of the good life.

The supposedly rich man who had approached her was Jules Dallagivanni, a dealer in the slave trade. Maximilien Baron, a long-time prostitute, had accompanied him. The trio sailed from France to New York. Almost immediately, Babut realized her awful dilemma. Closely guarded and verbally assaulted, she was never left alone by the two kidnappers. Babut was trapped.

From New York, the group traveled to Montana, where she was placed on the market as a prostitute in Missoula and Great Falls. A short time later, Dallagivanni and Baron took her to Los Angeles and put her in the "cribs" on Alameda Street.

The cribs on Alameda Street consisted of one-story brick buildings containing up to forty identical narrow rooms that weren't much wider than their doors. When not forced to have sex with customers, the women working the cribs stood in the doorways or just in front of the doors, waiting for the next trick. The scantily dressed women then invited customers to come inside. Saloons, gambling dens, and dance halls surrounded the cribs on Alameda Street. The area was crowded day and night, with people of many races hurrying from one dive to the next.

As the *Times* wrote about the tricks, "When the boys were flush with recent payrolls or winning streaks at poker or faro, they sought the sumptuous parlor houses of Commercial, New High, or Marchessault streets; but when their pockets were light, they had to be content with such feminine society as might be encountered in the cribs." The women sold their bodies an estimated thirteen to thirty times a night for around a dollar.

While the seventeen-year-old Babut was being forced into these dreadful conditions, her sister notified the police in Paris of Babut's disappearance. French officials alerted the United States and requested that her abductors be arrested and Babut return to Paris. The French would pay all expenses.

Months later, when word reached LAPD officials of her abduction, officers searched the cribs on Alameda Street. Discovering that the police were after them, the two kidnappers yanked Babut from her crib and hid in Santa

Monica, where the police quickly located them. Babut was taken into protective police custody and stayed with the family of an LAPD officer whose wife was French. Dallagivanni, constantly coughing with consumption, and the overweight Baron, wearing "cheap earrings dangling down to her shoulders," were arrested for importing Babut to the U.S. from France for immoral purposes.

Babut, a shell of her former self, then struggled with her experiences made worst when she had to testify against her kidnappers. Sitting with her abductors just a few feet in front of her in the courtroom, Babut took the witness stand. Frightened by the ordeal, she listened to words she could not understand until an interpreter was summoned. Still, the teenager sat traumatized in the federal courtroom staring into her lap with her head drooped, not wanting to make eye contact with anyone—especially her kidnappers. In the early twentieth century, attorneys on both sides did not handle these types of cases with anything amounting to sympathy. The questions were cold and to the point. Nothing was off limits.

As the questioning began, the abused French girl shrank from some of the questions. Then, gradually, she seemed to gain strength. Perhaps from the inspiration of several supporting women in the courtroom whose mission was to reform the crib district and rescue as many young girls as possible.

Babut was pressed hard by the defense attorneys, Mr. Davis and Mr. Rush. The men asked accusatory questions, such as why Babut didn't seek help from passing patrolmen. "Did you not know," they asked, "what the policemen are for?" Then unexpectedly, looking up briskly, Babut answered with a clear and strong voice, demonstrating her newfound confidence. "Oh, yes, sir, they are to protect everybody from harm," she answered innocently, But they did not know me from any other woman down there." One of the attorneys fired back, "Why did you not try to escape?"

"I was allowed nothing," she said, "but two scant dresses that came only to my knees: I had no other clothes. The other women were all watching me."

At the conclusion of the testimony, Judge Wellborn shocked most in the courtroom when he found the two defendants not guilty on a purely technical ruling. The judge said, "However deeply I may abhor and execrate the atrocious conduct of the defendants, I cannot allow myself for a moment to forget the law." Despite the ruling, Miss Baron was remanded to custody for other unrelated charges and spent years in prison. As for Dallagivanni, a few months after the trial he died of consumption.

Adolphine Babut remained in the United States and began earning a living under the tutelage of the women who had attended her trial and who encouraged the young woman never to give up.

Babut's situation was emblematic of a more significant problem. Progressivism also affected the police department. The Progressive Movement challenged those who operated businesses associated with vice for control of the city and, most importantly, the LAPD. The Progressives amended the city charter to include laws prohibiting anything to do with vice. Pushing back were the owners of the brothels, casinos, and saloons. The efforts of the reformers to eliminate prostitution, gambling, and drinking forced the entrepreneurs into politics, where they sought permissive council members. These vice lords' weapon of choice was bribery of politicians and members of the police force on a large scale.

The first outright victory by the progressives came in 1889 when they rewrote the city charter and established a police commission to supervise the police department. The first major accomplishment of the new commission was appointing John M. Glass as chief of police. The new chief held office from 1889 to 1900, a remarkable eleven years at a time when most chiefs lasted less than a year. Glass proved that when a chief was given tenure free from political involvement, positive and progressive results could follow.

Throughout more than a century and a half of LAPD history, two men stand at the peak of success for advancing a troubled police department: John Glass and, fifty years later, William H. Parker. While others have tried, and a select few have made positive contributions, these two chiefs pounded the nails into the framework of what LAPD is today.

Glass developed his political and law-enforcement skills as the marshal of Jeffersonville, Indiana, before becoming mayor in 1883. After two years, the forty-year-old headed to Los Angeles to lead a new group of citizens.

During Glass's term as chief, there was significant cooperation between progressive reformers and police management. The progressives respected modern technology to professionalize the police force. Chief Glass joined a newly established organization, the National (later International) Association of Chiefs of Police. From his earliest days, Glass embraced technology as the key to bringing the department out of mediocrity and elevating it into excellence. He was the first to introduce the idea of a professional police department, and he adopted technical improvements in transportation and communication. He emphasized being responsible, honest, and intelligent. He rewarded good job behavior with job tenure. Glass instilled camaraderie in the force but also instituted strict discipline. With his no-nonsense leadership, he made it clear that slacking off was unacceptable behavior.

In 1890, Glass addressed the political interference in the department in his first annual report to the mayor. He described the officer who looked to promote and receive favors by political favoritism:

> A political policeman is an unmitigated nuisance; the worst and most dangerous type of demagogue. He reasons from the false standpoint that the influence of the criminal classes is enough to control his position and promotion. Acting on this belief, he ignores every legal requirement of his office, and before he is aware of the fact himself, he becomes the sworn ally and partner of those who profit by violation of the laws of the land.

To better handle unusual occurrences (major disturbances in the city), Glass developed a "rifle squad," an early precursor to the SWAT team, which wasn't created for almost another seventy-five years. Armed with .45-70 caliber Winchester-repeating rifles, the sixteen-man squad, made up of volunteers, continually spent time drilling and in target practice. "I believe," said the chief, "that in certain emergencies the possession of these weapons and the knowledge of their use might be of great service to the city, while they add materially to the general appearance of the force on parade or inspection."

Glass also developed minimum qualifications for prospective officers. Applicants had to be twenty-five to thirty-five years old and have a chest of at least thirty-one inches. They also had to be at least five feet, eight inches tall. Borrowing a doctor from the United States Army, Glass required that each new patrolman pass a physical exam and have "sound limbs, perfect hearing, vision and speech. Not be a drunkard, write a good hand, and be fairly educated."

Reshaping the officers was important, but so was improving communication with patrolmen working all over the expanding city. Starting with just a single phone line for the entire police force, Glass adopted newly developed communication technology and added fifty Gamewell phones. Spread throughout LA, these phones were in metal boxes mounted on telephone poles and had a direct line to police headquarters. This allowed patrolmen to phone in every hour for security checks and receive calls for service from the station. Amazingly, these phones were still in use until the advent of the cell phone in the 1980s.

When Glass adopted the Bertillon identification system, he helped the police fight crime. The Bertillon system was first used in California. Before fingerprints, the system provided exact body measurements and photographs to identify and catalog criminals. The first year the department used the system, Glass stated in his annual report that the criminal element had been reduced by fifty percent.

Chief Glass also formed a detective bureau. In the LAPD's first two decades, there were no detectives. Patrolmen handled all aspects of an arrest and the investigation of all crimes. The likelihood of solving crimes significantly increased when the department added specialized detectives who investigated crime reports and trends.

An early department publication offers insight into how LAPD detectives were thought off:

> Only in story books is the detective a strange, one sided, mental gymnast, with bad habits, who can tell the name of a murderer by sniffing at the cigarette ash he has left on the scene of the crime. The real detective is a shrewd, zealous, pains-taking, hard-working policeman in citizen's clothes, who takes great risks at times and who occasionally is a principal in a thrilling man hunt, but who is far more often a very unromantic person simply

hanging on to a case until he reaches its conclusion.

Glass survived as chief of police for eleven years partly because he avoided any scandals involving vice. Criminals dealing in social evils continued to operate during his administration, but they did so with extreme caution. In his 1890 annual report to the mayor, Glass listed 212 lodging houses, 27 of "which are of doubtful reputation," 171 saloons, 65 poker rooms, 10 houses of prostitution, 89 cribs, 104 "prostitutes located and known," and 38 Chinese prostitutes. The LAPD made 2,575 arrests for the year.

Glass battled illegal activities with a stubbornness of a chief who would not allow them to rule the city. His competence limited the fuel for newspaper editorials and preachers who relished getting their congregations worked up over vice. If Glass got wind of vice occurring in the city, he attacked it with all means available. He understood this was the key to staying in office. The men who ran prostitution, gambling dens and orchestrated other vice activities did push back. Losing more and more money from Glass's attempt to shut down vice, his detractors made a concerted effort to rid themselves of this bothersome chief of police.

They attacked on several fronts. The Ministerial Union of Los Angeles led the charge, demanding that Glass resign because he was not suppressing vice in the city. Also attacking Glass: politicians, many of whom owned property in the profitable vice districts, and certain newspapers that wrote scathing editorials against the LAPD and its leader.

The leader of the Ministerial Union was the Reverend J.A.B. Wilson, who preached at First Methodist Church. The reverend insisted that "disorderly houses, poolrooms, and kindred dens of vice should be suppressed." He accused Glass of ineptitude and demanded his resignation. Glass fired back a broadside:

> Mr. Wilson is an unprincipled man who to secure a little cheap notoriety sought to break in to the newspapers by making statements which were unqualifiedly false…who had willfully distorted, perverted, misstated and misconstrued for the purpose of injuring me…[I] characterize it as the most outrageous act ever perpetrated by a man who wears the cloth. The whole committee should hide their faces in shame for allowing them to lie and be led by such a man.

As bombshells exploded around the longest-tenured chief in the history of the police department (at that time), the *Los Angeles Herald* published an editorial concerning the "reprehensible practice of the police department of locking people up and holding them for a day or more without a warrant or charge against them."

Noting the damage being done to Glass, Mayor Frederick Eaton chose the side of the naysayers. He accused Glass of "insubordination in losing his temper" and "talking back" to a police commissioner. Wounded by these battles, the LAPD's first genuinely professional chief relented to the pressure and retired on the last day of the nineteenth century. An editorial in the *Los Angeles Times* summed up the feelings of his supporters:

> Never, since the organization of a police department in the city of Los Angeles, have there been so few scandals therein as during the past ten years. This is not saying that Mr. Glass has not made mistakes, but it is saying that he is the best Chief of Police the city has had thus far in its history.

In 1900, Los Angeles was still a relatively small city of 102,000, but the vice, extortion, brutality, and inefficiency commonplace in larger Eastern cities now beset the City of Angels. Public discontent with the LAPD grew worse each year as the reformers fought to reorganize the department and get politicians to stop interfering with day-to-day operations. The police force was being batted back and forth like a ping pong ball—with the competing elements seeking control of the city.

Fearful of the rising crime rate, several businessmen and other professionals organized a Committee of Public Safety. They aimed to improve the LAPD by reforming those who oversaw the department. Consequently, their efforts did not start with the police department but were directed at the people sworn to support the force, the newly formed police commission.

In November 1900, the Committee for Public Safety published its report in the *Los Angeles Herald*. The results were stunning. According to the investigation, the newly formed police commission granted the city's Chinese gamblers immunity from prosecution in return for payoffs. For a price, the police commission issued licenses to operate saloons, allowing the proprietors to set illegal hours of operation, such as on Sundays, violating municipal liquor laws. The police board, at times, transferred honest patrolmen out of the vice district and put in questionable officers as replacements. Many of these men were debt-ridden, immoral, and unfit for a position of responsibility. Finally, the committee called on the community to turn the city council and police commission over to "honest men" regardless of political affiliation. That did not happen, but the progressives were not discouraged.

The Glass debacle added substance to a campaign for charter reform that began in 1902. A committee of bureaucrats and reform-minded citizens from the community successfully passed several amendments that directly impacted the LAPD.

The civil service amendment was awarded to every police officer except the chief and his secretary. The progressives hoped to finally establish the independence of the individual officer on the street and, more importantly, give the chief of police autonomy for the department's day-to-day operations. The amendment gave the chief legal authority to make substantial changes to the structure of the force. He could create or abolish divisions, remake policy to do what was best for the rank and file, and deploy police personnel for the good of the force.

The charter certified the minimum physical and mental entrance requirements, instituted competitive promotion examinations, and mandated salaries. The reformers failed, however, to include intelligence and personality prerequisites when testing police candidates.

The *Los Angeles Times* could not resist mocking the new exams designed for those applying to join the LAPD. The *Times* did this despite the fact that Captain Klener was administering the civil service exams. Klener, who was highly qualified, had served in the Austrian Army, the German Army, and the U.S. 7th Cavalry. He followed his army career by teaching at West Point Military Academy. In an editorial, the *Times* wrote:

> He [Klener] has been criticized because of his idea that policemen should have brains—a commodity of which the average policeman is beautifully innocent...The wooden stupidity of most of the men who have taken examinations for the police force in this city is absolutely wonderful...All that is required of a beat walker is to develop symptoms of an intelligence resembling in some degree that of a human being. Then he qualifies for a $10 a week job.

Few could have predicted that the civil service provisions in the 1902 charter amendments would have such an enormous impact on the city. The progressives could not resist writing their repugnance about vice into the law. The anti-vice campaign would influence politicians and the city for the next half-century. Corruption within city hall, the police force, and among many of the business elite in Los Angeles resulted from the underworld using whatever means necessary to prevent the reformers from taking control of Los Angeles and, thus, their pocketbooks. This was accomplished by intimidation, bribery, and through the elective process, by getting the votes necessary to eliminate them.

The man the reformers chose to take up the fight against organized vice was Charles Elton (1900–1904). His character was on display from the beginning. On the day he was selected to be chief, the 6-foot, 225-pound spry 45-year-old was driving a team of horses as the manager of the Los Angeles Transfer Company. Honing his management skills in the freight business, Elton took nine horses and a couple of wagons in his first year and quickly added to them, giving himself twenty-two wagons and seventy-six horses.

When an aide to the police commission tracked Elton down on a dusty side street and told him he had been elected chief and to report immediately to city hall, he said he was too busy. After some convincing, Elton reported for duty. Standing in front of the bureaucrats in his dusty, soiled clothes, he was asked what his strategy would be with the police force. Elton shrugged and replied that he had no idea. No matter, the first shot was fired in the war against organized vice. And the man holding the gun was the new chief.

Chief Elton's first action against vice was not expected by most—to keep the cribs open. This caused an uproar and war of words with Mrs. Chariton Edholm, the outspoken reformer from the Women's Christian Temperance Union, who, in conjunction with representatives from the Los Angeles City Union of Christians and the Los Angeles Ministerial Union, endeavored to close the cribs on Alameda Street.

The reformers blasted the wretched establishment of cribs in the city:

> The fires of indignation are burning white heat over the festering vice that continues like a cancerous sore, to exist in the confines of Chinatown, and to slough off into an ever-widening circle of disgusting wretchedness, touching and tainting new life-blood every day. Never has there been such an awakening on any subject as upon this of the crib.

The cribs and their inhabitants were best described in a letter to the *Times*:

> Here are rows of pens and narrow passages between them where buyers pass up and down. In the pens, exposed for

sale, are women, young and beautiful; they are very cheap and the market is open all night. Somewhere about the city are the unhung scoundrels who live in idleness and luxury upon the profits of this business.

While the progressives wanted the cribs shut down, the mayor and chief wanted them kept open. Chief Elton argued that by keeping the women in the cribs, the police could better maintain control. And by keeping them segregated, they could improve the safety and lifestyle of the rest of Los Angeles. Elton said:

In their attempt to restrict or abolish the practice of the oldest profession in the world, the reformers are trying to do something that never has been accomplished and in my opinion never will be. The evil should, and can be, controlled.

Elton believed that by centralizing the prostitutes in one area, the women could make a living without the threat of serious crime because there would be a heavy police presence.

Mayor Meredith Snyder agreed with his chief of police and fought against the reformers for trying to compel the officials "to do what we both believe to be the very worst thing for the city." The mayor, who would serve three different terms (1896-1921), argued that "thieving, stealing, in short, a carnival of vice and crime" would occur throughout the city if the cribs were shut down. Out of sight, out of mind was his logic.

The two leaders thought the prostitutes should be removed from public view, "and no one need see them or know of their existence unless he or she desires." Both leaders agreed they could close the cribs quickly and efficiently, but they warned of the consequences:

> These women must live-they must eat, they must have clothes, they must exist. If their business is taken away from them, they will stop at nothing to provide for themselves. Scattered all over town, the police department will be unable to watch them. Lodging houses will be infested...and they will get in the residence districts.

Of all the vice lords in the city, none was more pleased by the mayor and chief's opinions than Bartolo Ballerino, an Italian who had migrated to California during the Gold Rush. After arriving in Los Angeles, the future king of vice invested heavily in real estate, buying up the area around

Alameda Street. By the 1880s, and until he died in 1909, the man who earned the name of "crib king" owned most of the cribs, a saloon, and a restaurant that listed pimps, johns, and prostitutes as its best customers. Not that these criminals had any choice, as Ballerino forced them to frequent his establishments and to finance improvements to his buildings.

As with Adolphine Babut, the kidnapped seventeen-year-old French girl, women from around the world worked the cribs. Japanese, Chinese, African American, Belgian, Mexican, and Native American women had assigned areas with their own sets of pimps.

By 1903, with continual press reports supporting the progressives' desire to rid the area of the cribs, Alameda Street was about to get a makeover. Parting ways with Chief Elton, Mayor Meredith Snyder understood that something had to change, or he and the Democrats would get voted out of office in the next election.

The local press, which rarely agreed on anything, printed editorials supporting the crusades of the reformers and church groups. With newfound exuberance, church members blockaded the crib district, leaving the johns to look elsewhere for prostitutes. Other reformers went crib to crib to rescue those who wanted a new life, quickly getting the women into enclosed carriages and galloping them off to freedom.

With orders from the mayor, Chief Elton acquiesced and directed his men to start making arrests throughout Alameda Street. The first casualty was the "crib king" himself. Ballerino was arrested near one of his dives for renting a crib for prostitution. With Ballerino behind bars, the LAPD continued throughout the district, chasing away and arresting the hundreds who lived and worked there. The *Times* took immense pride in writing a haughty editorial about the raids:

> Darkness like a great mantle of charity settled down and softly stretched its folds of somber shadow over the erstwhile red-light district last night…The tenderloin was a deserted village. The 300 members of the demimonde who have been inmates of the cribs and stalls, had flown to escape the dragnet of the police and the stern justice of the city's courts. For the first time in the history of modern Los Angeles, the ribald jest, the vulgar song, the cheap and flashy show of finery on the be-painted and bespangled damsels…were not on exhibition for the gaze and gratification of the youths and men who seek such things.

Now, instead of twinkling red lights that were always a striking feature of these houses of "scarlet women," Alameda Street went dark as the last red light was extinguished. Ballerino died several years after his arrest. He went to his grave cursing the "damned old priest and preachers," the newspapers, and the "trouble-making women of the temperance's union."

Chapter 3

Civilian Chiefs of Police

"If I find a drone in the department, I will place him in the position of the man at sea in a leaky boat; he must either bail it out or drown."

—Edward F. Dishman, Chief of Police

The cycle of reform following a period of corruption became part of the LA landscape until 1950. The power struggle between the progressives and those in the vice business took turns running city hall and the police department. After Chief Elton successfully shut down much of the vice in the city, the underworld moved to remove him. Their chosen scheme was to start a rumor of corruption in the chief's office, which they knew would spread like cancer throughout the city. Once the vice lords disposed of the top cop, they would find a person more to their liking—a candidate who would permit the gamblers and others to do as they pleased without interference—all for a price of course.

The rumor mill was turned on in early 1904, and Chief Elton was gone by April. The accusations were of payoffs to specific individuals in city hall and the police force. Specifically, these officials were shaving money levied upon Chinese gamblers, prostitutes, and other underworld members.

To prepare for the criminals to run the city again, many crooks contributed money to a large purse that would go for future payoffs to men in the highest offices. Many former disgraced cops waited on the sidelines to be reinstated under the new administration, enabling them to enrich themselves through graft. In April, enough people believed the corruption rumors that Chief Elton was forced to retire. To the surprise of many, the hard-driving chief was never tried or convicted of any crimes.

The cycle of reform and corruption continued. Between 1904 and 1909, three LA mayors accused of misconduct were voted out of office. Five chiefs of police came and went, with their reputations seriously damaged by allegations of corruption. In 1904, Mayor Snyder lost his reelection bid to Owen McAleer, who earned the dubious nickname of "the whisky mayor" because he opposed saloon regulations. He was out after two years.

Vice again proved resilient despite the progressives' work to end it. Figueroa Street from Jefferson Street to Washington Street doubled as a racetrack, except there were no jockeys but scantily dressed prostitutes. One witness recalled: "As soon as the carriages reached Figueroa, they all turned and broke into a run…the girls standing up in the boxes of the hacks whooping and yelling, calling each other names and making bets on which team would win." Chasing after them were as many as fifty buggies driven recklessly by lustful young men. The reformers looked on, wondering what they must do to rid the city of such brazen displays of wickedness.

The progressives kept plugging away. While many of their reforms benefited the LAPD, others did not. The reformers reasoned that civilians should be at the head of the police department because they could better run the bureaucracy needed to move the police forward. The reformers failed to understand that without a sworn connection to the department or the camaraderie that Chief Glass had helped to instill, these outsiders were likely to be more obedient to the mayor who had appointed them than to the police force, whom they were strangers. Consequently, these civilians were often acquiescing "yes men" bowing to the mayor, who called the shots.

Edward Dishman (1909-1910) was a paradigm of this misplaced guidance. He was appointed chief and possessed all the characteristics of a man best suited for anything but the command of LAPD. Dishman had the support of the *Los Angeles Herald*, which reported, "Besides being eminently competent, he is 'white' clear through and square as a brick. There will be no graft in the chief's office while Dishman holds the job."

Behind the headlines lies the fact that Dishman was nothing more than an ordinary police reporter. He had no management or police experience. With their collective eyes on their man at the head of the LAPD, the *Herald*'s editorial writers exhorted, "He has gleaned in his capacity as police reporter, through long years of intimate association with officers, and has bred a valuable familiarity with the work."

Dishman's first remarks to a gathering of the rank and file offered insight into his politically motivated administration: "I'm going to give everyone a square deal. Past performances do not count with me...If I find a drone in the department I will place him in the position of the man at sea in a leaky boat; he must either bail it out or drown."

Priorities for civilian chiefs were quite different from those of their career counterparts. In one of his first actions as chief of police, Dishman did not go after flagrant vice in the city but instead asked the members of the horticultural commission to stop using poison to kill insects on strawberry plants, as people were getting sick.

Not surprisingly, Chief Dishman lasted only nine months. A report in the *Times* alluded to the fact that he "lost his place for lack of sympathy with the Reformers" and with the "good government forces in power." Failing to bail out his boat as he preached, Dishman departed to become the assistant postmaster of Los Angeles. The reformers would learn little from this experience and continued to put civilians in charge of the LAPD.

In the election of 1906, the progressives captured twenty-one of the twenty-three local offices they sought, but they lost the most desired prize. With support from the Southern Pacific Railroad, George Harper defeated reform candidate Lee C. Gates for mayor. The fun-loving playboy, who had an upper-class background, supported politician Joseph Edward Kern (1906–1909) as the next chief of police. The reform pendulum took a drastic swing back toward corruption. This corruption contributed to both men being forced from office in disgrace and one dying.

Chief Kern hailed from Iowa, leaving home as a teenager to head west. Early in his life, he was a teamster, hauling freight and then working as a laborer for the railroad.

He enlisted in the Army during the Indian Wars and was involved in the campaign to capture Chief Geronimo. Kern was discharged while living in California and found the area so appealing that he stayed. The three-hundred-pound Kern worked up the corporate ladder at the Los Angeles Ice and Cold Storage Company and became a shareholder. In 1902, Kern was elected to the Common Council and remained in that position until being appointed chief of police in November 1906.

Not long into the mayor's and chief's administration, an excitable, up-and-coming, fiery Southern attorney, thirty-four-year-old Thomas Lee Woolwine, blew the whistle on corruption in Los Angeles. He called out people in high places and became the darling of the reformers and the press.

Woolwine hailed from Nashville, Tennessee. He attended law school, clerked for two United States district attorneys, and was admitted to the California Bar in 1899. In 1907, Woolwine was appointed deputy city attorney of Los Angeles. One year later, he was named city prosecuting attorney. By virtue of that position, he also served as deputy district attorney of Los Angeles County.

He had been in office less than a year when the newcomer brazenly denounced his boss, John D. Fredericks, a country district attorney, as a "contemptible scoundrel."

Woolwine also labeled Chief Kern, Mayor Harper, and a police commissioner corrupt. Woolwine fed all his information to the *Los Angles Express,* which ran banner headlines such as: "Is Vice Protected?"

The millionaire owner of the *Express*, Edwin T. Earl, his associate editor, Edward Dickson, and a private detective conducted a personal investigation into vice in the city. Their much-publicized findings exposed payoffs, protection payments, stock fraud, influence-peddling and spotlighted the mayor's office, the police department, the police commission, and the board of public works. The new deputy city attorney was after anyone who had a stench of being dishonest.

The mayor, accused of being a crook, hurriedly redirected the press: "I have given orders to the police to close up the gambling joints, I am going to take personal charge now and see that these orders are carried out." And take charge he did. Reports in the *Examiner* alleged "His Honors" inspections of houses of ill fame turned into "orgies" and were anything but earnest investigations. When the *Los Angeles Express* refused to retract any stories, Mayor Harper hit them with a $600,000 lawsuit.

Chief Kern was accused not only of being involved with the prostitution syndicate but also of ordering members of the police department to harass the syndicate's competitors. Some in the gambling underworld just shrugged, as they had no fear of police interference. "It is easy to stand off the police in this affair," one crime boss said. "When I find that they are getting active, I just stop taking bets on the ponies for less than $50 because I know that the police can never get enough money ahead to put up so much to get evidence."

Prosecuting Attorney Woolwine encouraged District Attorney Fredericks to conduct a grand jury investigation into corruption within the city government. Fredericks told his subordinate that it was Woolwine's job to investigate and present evidence of the alleged dishonesty in City Hall to a grand jury. Letters between the two attorneys arguing about how to proceed flew back and forth in the newspapers.

"This is one of the gravest and most serious situations in your life," the DA exclaimed to Woolwine. Fredericks argued that he had never heard of corruption in City Hall or the police department but would back Woolwine's request for additional investigation funds. "Now, take off your coat and roll up your sleeves and get busy."

Threats to have Woolwine removed from office began circulating as soon as he pointed fingers at the mayor's office. But the young man would not be deterred. "Your inactivity during the course of many years of notorious official abuses in this city," Woolwine said to his boss, "is an indication that you, as my superior, would be absolutely unfriendly to any aggressive campaign for the purification" of the problem. Woolwine continued, "There is a condition in this city that makes it impossible for any conscientious prosecuting attorney to promptly discharge the duties of the office and I charge unhesitatingly that vice is being protected in this city by the mayor and police commission and that I have sufficient evidence" to prove it. He ended his letter by accusing the DA of being "cowardly" and afraid to form a grand jury to pursue these allegations.

The district attorney had had enough of his brazen subordinate. Fredericks summoned Woolwine to his office and fired him. The DA justified his decision to the press: "I listened to him carefully for some hours and thoroughly satisfied myself that the young man, however earnest, is thoroughly incompetent for such important work."

The grand jury eventually investigated the allegations Woolwine presented and those made by the *Los Angeles Express*. The grand jury, controlled by Fredericks, investigated and found one-hundred brothels in operation. It also alleged that the mayor and one member of the police commission owned hotels and other rental properties in the segregated vice zone. That saloon keepers had been persuaded to buy $250,000 worth of stock in Harper's oil and sugar business. Further, the grand jury found that Chief Kern directed a firm that sold fire insurance to local businesses, especially those requiring a city license. When all was done, the grand jury found evidence that brothels were in operation but could not find corroborative evidence of protected vice.

Despite the grand jury's ruling, the *Los Angeles Star* continued to print headlines condemning both chief executives for corruption. The press was too much for Chief Kern, who resigned and was replaced by his vice commander, Captain Thomas Broadhead (1909). Three years after retiring, Kern, an alcoholic, traveled to El Paso, Texas, checked into a hotel, went to the bathroom, got into the bathtub, and shot himself in the temple. The LAPD did not send anyone to his funeral. A petition to recall Mayor Harper forced the mayor to resign. Woolwine eventually replaced his former boss as county district attorney and pursued corruption in city hall until he ran a losing bid for California governor years later.

From 1900 to 1909, seven chiefs of police held office, but only two came from within the LAPD. The chiefs from the police department best represented the career officers' desire to professionalize the department. Having to tolerate these constant changes at the top, professional police officers were difficult to retain. Veteran officers did what they had to to survive until the civilian chief was fired or quit, and the occasional chief from within the department took command.

In an ongoing trend, the police were outnumbered and outgunned. City Hall obstructed the fight against spiraling crime and hardline gangsters who were protected by politicians who allowed crime to thrive—doing so because they could make money from the criminal activities. For the next half-century, LA was a hotbed for prostitution, illegal alcohol, gambling, and vice because politicians restricted the police department's effectiveness. The police were told whom they could shake down and when they should look the other way as City Hall flexed its full authority over the police force. Politicians appointed and dismissed officers at will. Police morale fell to new lows.

During the early 1900s, crooks once again stormed Los Angeles like a herd of stampeding cattle during the Wild West days. This time they didn't arrive riding horses; they drove fancy automobiles and wore expensive suits. They were the new emerging professional criminal.

The charter revision of 1911 further solidified this protocol. The charter replaced the five-member police commission with a three-member nonpartisan board composed of the mayor and two appointees acceptable to the city council. But the new charter went even further in giving the mayor authority over the LAPD. The mayor now had complete control to appoint, direct, and dismiss the chief of police. In a short twenty-two-year span, command of the police department had passed from the city council, through the hands of the police commission, and into the control of a single elected official—the mayor.

Because of the lack of solid leadership in the chief's office, the low pay, and much in-fighting, corruption within the ranks became a recurring nightmare. When Chief Kern resigned, Captain Broadhead took command but lasted a scant four months. Broadhead resigned after he was indicted for accepting bribes—not unlike his former boss. The citizens' respect for the Los Angles Police Department was now at its nadir.

During another grand jury investigation, Nick Oswald, a prominent LA gangster who ran the red-light district, was granted immunity for his testimony concerning corruption in City Hall. Oswald explained to a prosecuting attorney about a meeting he had with Broadhead. Broadhead had demanded a payoff of $1,000. "Well, I need the money damn bad," the chief had said. "I have a ranch to pay for, and I need the money." The gangster responded, "I can't pay it now, but I will pay you $250 a week during the month if that will help you out." He knew street cops made $18 a week. Broadhead agreed.

After he was found out, Broadhead resigned as chief but was amazingly not fired. Instead, the new chief, ex-newspaper reporter Edward Dishman (1909–1910), gave him his previous rank of captain. George Alexander, the seventy-year-old freshly elected mayor, defended his decision. "We are all free from prejudice in the matter, and the future will take care of itself. We will not be parties to any injustice, and Broadhead takes his old place just as if no question had been raised."

A short time later, Captain Broadhead was indicted of bribery. After a lengthy trial, he was acquitted but had become too hot a commodity to remain on the LAPD. His tarnished career was over.

In all my research, one article stands out for excellence in identifying the problem with LAPD and provided suggestions to correct them. In April 1909, when Chief Broadhead resigned and the next civilian chief, Edward Dishman, was taking command, the *Los Angeles Times* wrote an editorial titled, "What's the Matter with Our Police?" The newspaper perceptively identified the problems within the LAPD. The *Times* pointed out that the force was severely demoralized, and discipline was nowhere to be found. "The new chief will find his little army eaten through and through with intrigues, undermined by cliques, conspiracies, secret factions trying to undo one another—a network of political wires supposed to render certain sets of police officers immune to discipline. He will find patrolmen arrayed in feuds...."

The author suggested the police department needed to be "shaken" until its members no longer dared to scheme against the political bosses or one another. Instead, they should "have their hands full trying to escape the wrath of someone whom they thoroughly fear." The author suggested that the police force was essentially a military organization and that the LAPD was demoralized because it departed from the "military principles."

> The men have come to regard the Chief as an official whose hands are absolutely tied and who is sure to lose his job before long-in fact, as a rather unfortunate "goat" being fattened for the slaughter. They have come to regard the members of the police commission as their real masters, and to regard these commissioners as being swayed more by political considerations than by desire to enforce impartial military discipline. The

patrolman should be made to understand that the sergeant of his watch and the lieutenant of his district are, to him, final and absolute; that he may not carry any matters to higher officers without explicit permission of his immediate superiors. Most of all, social gossip between officers and men must cease at once. It is absolutely essential that a wide gulf be created between the rank and file and those in authority.

It is vital that he stand aloof from his officers and that to him, the new chief shall be the great, unapproachable terror-striking god-of-the-dump whose rebukes he fears and whose praise, through the formal distance of police bulletins, is a coveted honor.

Almost no one in the department listened to the *Times* suggestions, primarily because politicians interfered with how the LAPD was managed. But the *Times* had hit on something; some forty years before, O.W. Wilson had set the standard for the professionalism movement within law enforcement. In the 1950s, in his book *Police Administration*, which was the blueprint for professional policing, he wrote that there must be an emphasis placed on a military-style organization with the accompanying level of discipline.

By 1909 the population of Los Angeles had swelled to 300,000. The LAPD had just 336 officers on the streets policing them. There was one officer for every 5,803 Angelinos. By contrast, San Francisco had a much smaller area to patrol and had 913 patrolmen—nearly three times as many as LA. Still, twice as many criminals were convicted in Los Angeles as in San Francisco. The *Times* noticed: "That criminals have learned to fear, and even if the force remains one-third as large as it should be, they most likely will profit by the department's excellent record and give Los Angeles a wide berth." The LAPD has struggled with a shortage of police officers throughout its history. Police chiefs almost constantly cried out for additional patrolmen. As one chief put it:

> When you attempt to carry a two-ton load on a one-ton truck you cannot hope to transport the load properly...you have breakdowns...The most highly trained efficiency expert can never devise a way to performing the physically impossible task of having one man simultaneously in three different places, and that is about what we are trying to do with things as they are.

Another area where the progressives failed with their charter reforms, beyond the shortage of officers, was what the officers could put in their pockets—their salaries. These were two reasons civilians did not want to pin on a badge. Consequently, few desirable men applied. In 1910, the pay for a patrolman was a meager $75 a month; a milkman made more. All of this would change, at least in the short term, when International Iron Workers' Union members dynamited the *Los Angeles Times* building, killing twenty-one innocent employees and wounding one hundred more. In the anti-radical hysteria that followed, the police force was raised to five-hundred men, and officers got a bump in pay.

Overall, the progressives' influence on the LAPD reorganized the political pressure. The reformers emphasized proper police administration without undue political influence, which meant that the word "professionalism" began to creep into the vocabulary of some observers and in police circles. It was sorely needed.

The progressives' fight against organized vice expanded as the police department was under less political pressure from time to time. Clergymen became more vocal, as many were sworn in as special "constables" to root out vice in the city. The Morals Efficiency League made up of clergymen, abolished many forms of gambling, including betting on horse races and prize fights. To address prostitution, the reformers passed an ordinance forbidding sexual intercourse between persons not married to each other. This law was short-lived; it was ruled unconstitutional, and, in the end, only a few unfortunate lovers were convicted of adultery or fornication.

Despite the attempts of these do-gooders, vice survived by hiding in the city's crevices, ready to come out when the proper political circumstances arose. For Los Angeles, the ongoing cycle of reform and corruption would haunt the corridors of City Hall and the chief's office for the next four decades.

Chapter 4

Politics and the Battle Between Reform and Corruption

"I have stated before that the police department was not in politics. Any active participation in politics by any member of the police department will mean instant dismissal. This is emphatic and final; there will be no deviation or exception made."

—Charles E. Sebastian, Chief of Police

It was a night to remember. While a substantial bonfire burned, thousands of supporters gathered for Chief of Police Charles Sebastian (1911–1915). They didn't gather because he was chief. He was very popular, but it was more than that. Most citizens were there to support the man they wanted to be elected as their next mayor. With the election just days away, the assemblage of voters wanted to close out the mayoral campaign with a vast motor parade. Idling along two miles of roadway was a line of automobiles with banners hung from their shiny doors. The signs had bold headlines inviting citizens to elect "Charles Sebastian, the People's Candidate for Mayor."

Hundreds waved from the sidewalks as the procession snaked through the business district. With horns honking, the noise amplified by the surrounding buildings, Chief Sebastian and his wife led the parade just as he had led the police department for the past four years.

When the procession stopped, the press caught up with the chief to get his comments. Although tired, he spoke loud enough for most to hear: "I ask for election as mayor because I believe I have had that experience which equips and qualifies me to hold the position. I do not want to be elected if the people do not believe I can efficiently handle the city's affairs as mayor." The perfect announcement for the gambling crowd. Bets were quickly taken as to who would win the mayor's race and how many votes the winner would receive. Like all other vices, gambling was as natural to LA as sunshine.

Charles E. Sebastian's career became a momentary bright spot for the city. Appointed as chief in 1911, Sebastian won a temporary stay against the vice lords by running a "clean" police department and teaming up with the powerful progressives. The chief supported efforts by a small group of reformers, led by local preachers, to eliminate gambling and prostitution from the streets of Los Angeles. The reformers faced challenges from underworld figures who wanted to protect their illegal businesses and found it in their best interest financially to support the opposing political groups. In past years, these corrupt vice lords and politicians controlled the city, and any police chief who attempted to eliminate them often read in the newspapers of his early retirement. Between 1915 and 1923, four mayors and eight chiefs of police held office. In every case, a vice scandal forced them out.

Sebastian, a handsome man from Missouri who had fought in the Spanish-American War, joined the police department in 1900. He gave credibility to the theory that having a career police officer run the department was best for the city and those the department employed. He rose quickly through the ranks by earning a reputation as an incorruptible, often raiding vice establishments in Chinatown. Sebastian's success can be traced to his pedigree; his father and grandfather were deputy sheriffs. Watching these men perform their duties reasonably without compromise, the young Sebastian had learned the traits of solid law enforcement, which served him well in the mean streets of LA.

Charlie Sebastian gained notoriety for his remarkable rise from patrolman to chief to mayor. No one before or since has ever held all three positions. His subsequent devastating spiral to complete failure adds a footnote to Los Angeles history that's hard to grasp today.

Sebastian was awarded the position of chief for his work ethic, not because he was an obedient "yes man" to the leaders in City Hall. He was a natural leader. He was able to propel the LAPD forward without the mayor interfering because he worked to keep politics out of the department's day-to-day operations:

> I have stated before that the police department was not in politics. I repeat that statement now. Any active participation in politics by any member of the police department will mean instant dismissal. This is emphatic and final; there will be no deviation or exception made.

Three days after taking office, Chief Sebastian addressed the subject of promotions, having seen so many officers promoted over him not for their ability as patrolmen but because of their political connections.

> Promotions will be made according to the merits of the man in question. If there is any officer present who thinks a little

political pull is going to help him gain promotion, he had better change his mind immediately, for I can promise you that political influence will not count with me. Every man who rises from the ranks while I am chief will have shown that he is a competent man for the new office.

Just as Chief Glass had in the 1890s, Chief Sebastian proved that enormous strides could be made to professionalize operations without political interference in the police department. In his own words, Sebastian was most gratified for his municipal farm. From experts in the field of alcohol abuse, he had learned to treat drunkards not as criminals but as human beings with ailments affecting them both mentally and physically. Letters of gratitude poured in from most inmates who went through the system. In his annual report to the mayor, Sebastian wrote, "Replenished with new hope, their bodies built up and their minds cleared, these men can now face life with a courage they themselves had counted lost." Homeless inebriates were sentenced to his farm instead of jail. Sebastian ensured they received rehabilitation through plenty of exercise, food, and work. The functioning farm grew crops used to feed the prisoners in jail.

As a reform-minded chief, Sebastian oversaw twenty ministers appointed as special police officers to improve the lives of those on the streets. The chief purchased an automobile that he converted into a police ambulance, conceptually way ahead of its time. He recruited young graduate physicians to staff the new emergency vehicle, not unlike the paramedics of today. He assigned a "flying squad" to be posted at Central Station and had them in reserve if he needed them for unusual occurrences or to supplement patrol officers.

The innovative chief saw the need for a law that would regulate the speed of motor vehicles and for a law to register cars once a year to track ownership. Sebastian pushed for a driver's examination that applicants must pass before being granted a driver's license. He required hospitals to report traumatic injuries, which assisted the police in investigating violent crimes.

He envisioned a citizen police force that nearly mirrors today's police reserves. From the city council, he asked for funding for five hundred of LA's best citizens to assist the police department in controlling crime. More than one thousand applied. These unpaid citizen officers were able to make arrests and work the streets with their sworn counterparts.

With over four years of success on the job, the popular chief decided that he could further serve the citizens of Los Angeles as their mayor. Sebastian soon learned about genuine city politics in the weeks leading to the election. While the underworld put up with Sebastian as chief, they did not want to see him as the top executive in LA. The criminals went after Sebastian in a mudslinging campaign that reddened the faces of the reformers who supported him.

The underworld harassed the chief on all fronts. Sebastian was indicted in the death of a homeless man. He was accused in the press of contributing to the delinquency of a minor. On the eve of the election, someone attempted to assassinate the chief by firing two shots at him while he was dining in his home. To the disbelief of almost the entire city, Sebastian was arrested and put in the slammer for allegedly arranging his own assassination! Although these allegations made great headlines, all charges against the chief were eventually dropped. In one of the ultimate political reversals, Sebastian's criminal foes were blamed, and the chief landed in the mayor's office. But it would be a love affair that would be the downfall of the new mayor.

Mayor Sebastian hardly tried to keep it a secret that he had a mistress named Lillian Pratt. While on an official trip with his wife, Elsie, Sebastian wrote his mistress several love letters, wishing she was there with him instead of the "old hay bag," and then forgot to mail them. His wife found the revealing letters and, to get revenge, handed them over to the press. After over a year in office, the resulting fallout ended Mayor Sebastian's political career. He never recovered. Blacklisted as a sinning adulterer in the reformist-run Los Angeles, the former chief and mayor could find only odd jobs, such as a gas station attendant. After a devasting stroke in 1929, the fifty-six-year-old Sebastian died in a Venice bungalow with his lover by his side.

Following Sebastian's removal, dishonest city officials saw an opportunity to appoint their people to his and several other executive positions. Unfortunately, many of these new appointees meshed politics and policing so completely that Los Angeles again became a breeding ground for corruption—casting a dark shadow over the department that did not lift for decades.

With Sebastian gone, the political machine in Los Angeles would force the pendulum of change to swing quickly away from reform and toward outright corruption. Police departments across the United States in the late nineteenth century and early twentieth century were firmly entrenched in the day-to-day affairs of big-city politics. For a price, many law enforcement officers provided services and assistance to political allies. They harassed, arrested, and interfered with the political activities of their adversaries. The politicians and business elite ran or supervised gambling, prostitution, drug distribution, and racketeering. It was difficult to separate the political parties and organized crime. In most large cities, they were one and the same.

The progressives, fighting back, supported candidates they believed stood for their Midwestern puritanical hatred of any form of vice. But the opposing vice establishment was constantly adapting. As the tide of corruption threatened to sweep over the reformers, they became more determined. In part, they regained power by supporting candidates that were proven progressives in all areas of city government. Their platform was simple: To defeat corruption.

To fill the remainder of Mayor Sebastian's term, the city council elected Frederick T. Woodman, a childless widower of forty-seven. To finance his 1919 bid for mayor, Woodman searched for funding—"the mother's milk of politics." For chief of police, Woodman chose John L. Butler (1916–1919), a career officer, to replace C.E. Snively (1915–1916), an ex-newspaperman and Sebastian's former secretary. In his annual report to the mayor in 1919, Butler concisely stated the coming political firestorm: "During the few months prior to the city election on June 3, the department was vigorously assailed." It began with the search for funding and ended with the mayor's arrest for "asking and receiving a bribe." The subsequent grand jury highlighted the corruption in City Hall and the LAPD.

Mayor Woodman chose Horace Karr, a former *Los Angeles Times* reporter, as his closest adviser and charged him with acquiring funding for the campaign. As was the standard during this era, Karr went to the vice lords. But Karr found the pickings slim, with the cribs closed and the criminals laying low from the reformers. Karr was not deterred. He knew the men to contact from his days of reporting on vice. George Brown and George Henderson were two "negro" patrolmen and veterans of the days when cribs were rampant, and enterprising dirty cops could score lots of money. Patrolmen Brown and Henderson ran several gambling houses and bordellos and sold liquor violating the Gandier ordinance, a municipal law banning alcohol during wartime. All their vice activity took place in Black establishments.

The policemen arranged a deal with Karr: for $25,000 a month ($362,000 in today's money), Brown and Henderson would supply the funds for the Woodman campaign in exchange for protection from the vice squad when he was elected. The corrupt cops wanted either to be warned when raids were going to take place or to put Sergeant William "Wild Bill" Hackett in charge of the unit. The payment was to be monthly until the election was over.

In March 1919, the county grand jury indicted Woodman, Karr, Brown, Henderson, Sergeant Hackett, and three other patrolmen. Immediately after the indictment, Mayor Woodman was arrested and booked—not ideal for his bid to win reelection. Meeting with the press as he was bailed out of jail, the mayor was relaxed and stated his innocence. "Such accusations are to be expected at the beginning of a campaign."

During testimony in the subsequent trial, Karr, the former reporter, casually (appalling today) talked of how he raised money for the campaign. "I got the money from Chinks, some from the Japs, and a little from the niggers." He elaborated, "From the Chinks we can get large sums of money. The Japs won't pay much, and the niggers don't make much." His racist comments are revolting but demonstrate the prevailing thought among many in early twentieth-century Los Angeles.

Sergeant Hackett, feeling the pressure, wanted insulation from his chief of police. He told Karr, "Butler and I don't get along well. The mayor ought to be strong enough to prevent Butler from interfering with me." In further testimony, he accused Mayor Woodman of getting rid of people in the police department who might interfere with him when he was elected. The mayor said Chief Butler was a good policeman but had no political sense and was "not a good man for the place."

In the typical political inclination of the day, neither the mayor nor the rest involved in this trial was found guilty. Woodman had steadfastly denied all knowledge of Karr's misdeeds. Karr and Brown had received immunity and testified against the mayor. While the police officers had been acquitted, they were by no means exonerated. The trial testimony clearly established the existence of protected vice in Los Angeles. George Henderson had refused to talk and was convicted. But when supposed "new evidence" surfaced, a second jury failed to reach a verdict. District Attorney T. L. Woolwine consequently withdrew all charges against Henderson, questioning why the little man should go to prison while the mayor went free. Woodman returned to the campaign trail but lost to Meredith Pinxton "Pinky" Snyder, who received 61 percent of the vote.

It appears that Chief Butler failed to detect the corruption under his command, which is strange, considering he was known to be a strict enforcer of the law. In his three years as chief, he investigated 371 officers for misconduct. Of those, the chief gave eighty that had disgraced the department a choice: either resign or be fired. In July 1919, Chief Butler announced his decision to resign as chief and revert to his previous rank of captain, where he served another three years. He died in 1945.

By 1920, by which time Los Angeles had grown to 576,000, its inhabitants had little to drink. The wartime liquor prohibition began under the municipal Gandier Act in 1916. It was quickly followed by the Eighteenth Amendment to the U.S. Constitution, which prohibited the manufacture, sale, and transportation of alcoholic beverages. The Volstead Act was passed to carry out the new amendment. Together these new acts and amendments produced a law enforcement crisis of unprecedented dimensions. Opportunities for graft exceeded anything previously known. Policemen and politicians, all eager to benefit from the new-found opportunities involved in liquor production, pushed one another aside as the profits grew and grew.

Chapter 5

Prohibition
Angels Awash in Alcohol

"Every hoodlum should show his gratitude by wearing a medallion of the Volstead Act around his neck."

—Los Angeles rum runner

The Woman's Christian Temperance Union, better known as the WCTU, sought a "sober and pure world." They came in droves—women of all ages carrying their axes in one hand and their prohibition signs in the other. They were at LAPD headquarters to protest against the evils of drinking and to ensure that the demon liquor in police custody was indeed being destroyed. The spiritual group had zero tolerance for what they deemed to be the wickedness of liquor and fought against alcohol being used in any way, including wine in religious ceremonies. How could the church use wine, they argued, when it contained "the narcotic poison, alcohol, which cannot truly represent the blood of Christ."

When the court ordered the confiscated liquor destroyed, the women arrived at Central Station standing as sentinels to ensure the LAPD officers did their job. With so many onlookers, the department treated the disposal as an official police ceremony. A sergeant stood at attention, overlooking the patrolmen as each barrel of illegal booze was carefully marched out and poured down the drain. As each barrel was dumped, the ladies cheered and waved their signs in celebration. But what the women missed in their festivity was the slight smirk on some of the officers' faces.

LAPD's Central Station was constructed and occupied in the summer of 1896 during Chief Glass's term. The station remained in operation for a staggering sixty years. When first built, the building towered fifty feet above all nearby structures. It was not a beauty by any means, but it had one interesting decorative element. Central Station had large hand-chipped gray stone blocks outlining perfect arches above the windows. That was the only time anyone would've described the police headquarters as perfect.

As the *Los Angeles Herald* reported, "When the building was completed and moved into, it was found to be arranged for almost any other kind of place than a police station." The building was so poorly designed that it had to be completely remodeled after just a few years.

Despite all its shortcomings, Central Station served its purpose for a select few patrolmen in one overlooked area— a plain old drain. Back in the horse-and-buggy days, a driveway had been built for the wagons. The driveway was on the ground floor at the building's east end. Their wagon in tow, the horses were driven into the building and onto a bulky turntable. The wagon would be unhitched, the horses removed, and the turntable rotated around to pick up a fresh set of horses. These horses were hitched to the wagon so the policemen could be off to the next call with fresh mounts.

During Prohibition, scheming patrolmen came up with an ingenious idea. Located in the center of the turntable was a drain used for run-off as the men washed down the wagon just before it went back onto the streets. With the advent of the automobile, the police no longer had use for the turntable, and it was removed, but the drain remained. The patrolmen were careful to keep it clean.

Under the watchful eyes of the WCTU and, at times, the mayor and other dignitaries, patrolmen diligently poured the illegal liquor down the drain. The officers were cautious in pouring just one barrel at a time, careful not to mix wine or beer with the hard liquor.

As the liquor disappeared into the rerouted drain, it traveled underground down the sloping hill to a rear room in a nondescript building on the west side of Broadway. Awaiting the gushing liquor, off-duty patrolmen quickly and efficiently filled empty barrels with the valuable liquor, rebottled it and sold it to their favorite bootleggers. When it was over, everyone was delighted to see that the court's order was fulfilled, with thousands of gallons of illegal alcohol destroyed—as everyone thought. Welcome to Prohibition Los Angeles, where most had a plan to usurp the Eighteenth Amendment.

Prohibition was proposed in December 1917. Nebraska was the thirty-sixth state to ratify the amendment on January 16, 1919, when the Eighteenth Amendment became law. It was implemented one year later, on January 17, 1920. Over the objections of President Woodrow Wilson, Congress passed the Volstead Act, which provided enforcement powers for the alcohol ban.

As clocks struck midnight on January 17, the law targeting Americans' love affair with alcohol would profoundly impact the nation. As the Eighteenth Amendment became law, everyday events, such as taking a bottle of wine to a friend's house for dinner or just sipping a drink in public, were now illegal from coast to coast.

Violators of the law faced up to six months in jail and a fine of up to $1,000.

For those citizens who would not give up their right to drink, their new life as criminals happened in small increments. It went from bathtub hooch to a basement still, from handing out bottles of homebrew to friends to providing beer to a few strangers. It happened so quickly and so subtly that the cops and politicians paid little attention in the beginning. Prohibition made criminals of almost the entire population. The "dry" paradise that the prohibitionists envisioned became a breeding ground for bootleggers, racketeers, and speakeasies, all eager to sell to a thirsty public.

But not everyone was thirsty, and the "drys" continued to preach about the evils of alcohol and how the world would be different after January 17. In Virginia, the Reverend Billy Sunday, a professional baseball player turned evangelist, went so far as to conduct a funeral for "John Barleycorn."

> Good-bye John! You were God's worst enemy; you were hell's best friend....The reign of tears is over, the slums will soon be only a memory. We will turn our prisons into factories and our jails into storehouses and corncribs. Men will walk upright now, women will smile, and the

children will laugh. Hell will be forever
for rent.

Wartime liquor prohibition under the municipal
Gandier Act in 1916, followed by the Eighteenth
Amendment, produced a crisis of unprecedented
dimensions. The opportunities for graft exceeded anything
previously known. As profits soared, the proportion of
policemen, politicians, and criminals eager to share in the
bonanza took off. Vice now looked like small potatoes
compared with the liquor business.

The new racketeers were the recipients of the most
significant break any small-time criminal could have hoped
for. Banning alcohol drove crime to heights no one could
have imagined. As one rum runner suggested, "Every
hoodlum should show his gratitude by wearing a medallion
of the Volstead Act around his neck."

New blood entered the rackets, including college men
who had plenty of brains and were eager to make millions.
These young upstarts showed the old-time thugs how to
operate nationally and better ways to get rich. Fighting
against this new gold rush, the LAPD floundered as it
attempted to keep its head above water. As Prohibition
began, LAPD was drowning.

Chapter 6

Corruption Everywhere

"POLICE STENCH GROWS WORSE: The *Record* is forced to resume exposure of rotten, graft-ridden police conditions forced to do so by the mass of police corruption which grows worse with the passing of the weeks and months."

—*Los Angeles Record*

Ushering in the Roaring Twenties was Chief George K. Home (1919–1920), a fifteen-year veteran of the department who learned much from his father, John, who had been one of the first detectives in the LAPD. Home was promoted quickly, earning further experience as a deputy chief under Chief Snively. The junior Home was a quiet man who carried a big stick. On one of his first nights as a patrolman, he broke his club over a mugger's head in Chinatown.

Appointed to chief by Mayor Meredith Snyder, Home was one of the earliest chiefs to adopt a transparency policy for the LAPD. "At the time I accepted this office, I announced that the Department would pursue an open-door policy." He continued: "Nothing has been hidden from the public, and the press, the eye, and voice of the citizenry, has been given free access to all the work of the department."

Despite Home's openness, Home's administration faced a series of occurrences that produced what he called "a breakdown of social restraint." Violent liquor wars and widespread public crime marked the struggle against Prohibition lawbreakers. Anarchists, Communists, and the leaders of the Industrial Workers of the World were, as Home saw it, at war against the American way of life. Chief Home continually sought to rally his officers through bold headlines in the police *Daily Bulletin* (something rarely done). "IMMEDIATELY HALT ALL UNPATRIOTIC AND RADICAL MOVEMENTS." He directed officers to study "carefully" the Syndicalism Act and immediately stop anti-American meetings, radical gatherings, and unpatriotic speeches. "Use every effort to stamp out the 'Red' movement. To halt all street speaking and gatherings and dispense and disperse the assembled sympathizers. Prosecute these lawless persons to the full extent of the law." To support his officers, he formed an anarchist squad and a bomb squad that specialized in activities brought on by the "radicals."

Efforts to thwart the problems Prohibition created continued during his fourteen months as chief. However, Home did not lose track of the critical need to suppress vice activities in the city. Using the *Daily Bulletin*, he instructed his men to report every house suspected of being disreputable or where gambling might occur. Officers were to report the abuses to their commanding officers immediately. Failure to do so would result in suspension. He directed the divisional captains to present their reports to the chief in person.

But a hole in his veil of public proclamations appeared shortly after Home became chief. Like other chiefs, Home rehired twelve ex-policemen dismissed for serious offenses such as theft, assault, and bribery. He put some of these men in positions of authority over incumbent officers. The chief argued that these men deserved second chances after proving to be exceptional citizens in the community. Two former policemen who could not get past the civil service requirements were put on his personal "secret service" payroll. One, Herbert "Brute" Kittle, earned his nickname by beating prisoners. He had been fired four years earlier. The other was Harry J. Raymond, a disgraced former LAPD officer who was a model for a corrupt policeman. Raymond had talked the good folks of Venice, California, into hiring him as their chief of police. After being sued, charged with false arrest, and fighting with subordinates, he was indicted for extortion. The DA had thought he had an airtight case until his star witness fled the state after having his life threatened. The case was not tried, but Raymond was unceremoniously fired. He would later star in one of the LAPD's most bizarre corruption cases.

As for Brute Kittle, he was killed by gunfire. The events leading to his death began unfolding just after midnight on a Friday in the detectives' office at police headquarters. Kittle, obviously inebriated, was there. Also present: Fire Commissioner Frankenstein; Emmett Dalton, "a reformed train bandit"; Patrolman George Ryan; Ben Haddoz; C. R. Wertz; Hiram Wambold, police secretary under Chief John Butler's regime; A. M. Rochlen and R. S. Edwards, reporters for the *Los Angeles Times*; and a dozen other men—twenty witnesses to what was to happen.

Kittle was spurting off his mouth to anyone who would listen. He complained about an expose published by the *Record* that identified him and eleven other ex-cops as having been hired by Chief Home despite their previous misdeeds. "I made the *Record* shut up once before," he boasted, "and I can do it again." The new secret service cop also had words for the mayor. "They hired me, but they can't none of them fire me. Mayor Snyder tried it and couldn't get away with it. I'm backed up by the Big Four Brotherhoods."

To emphasize his point, Kittle whipped out his automatic pistol and shot four holes in the floor, right next to the feet of Mr. Wambold, the former police secretary. Several who were present later suggested that Kittle was trying to show off for Emmett Dalton, the former train robber. Acting as calm as can be expected with the roar of a pistol just a few feet from where he was sitting, Dalton yawned several times as if bored with the whole act. With a wall preventing Mr. Wambold from running from the party, he put a big smile on his face and lit a cigar, albeit with trembling hands.

With everyone's ears still ringing, Kittle jumped up and stormed into Lieutenant George Daudel's office. Daudel tried to calm the still-armed man, and Kittle, slurring his words, complained that Chandler of the *Times* would publish something derogatory about his criminal friends, Al Jennings and Emmett Dalton. He said that while the paper had in the past called them out for their "badness," Kittle thought he was "badder." He fired several more bullets into the floor next to the lieutenant to prove his point. That was enough. Two officers present grabbed Kittle and escorted him to the street. He was told if he returned, he would be locked up. He kept his gun.

The department was embarrassed one of their own had shot up police headquarters and said Kittle's actions were a prank and that Kittle was only shooting blanks. The two reporters who witnessed the rampage made it clear in the newspaper that it was the real deal, and one had only to go to the detectives' office and look at the bullet holes in the floor to be convinced.

Days later, Kittle bragged to those around him that he had too many powerful friends to be fired. Wrong. Kittle was again fired from the LAPD. A subsequent investigation into his corrupt ways found evidence in his desk that tied him to several robberies. As the LAPD closed in on his home to arrest him, Kittle fired one more shot—into his head.

Home's rehiring of disgraced officers such as Raymond and Kittle can be traced back to the men's direct relationship with organized crime in Los Angeles. If incumbent officers would not work as "bag men" collecting dirty money, the criminals hired those who would. The crooks, police, politicians, and business elite who ruled the underworld ensured no competing criminal operation succeeded. They accomplished this by orchestrating police raids against those outside their group. During Home's term, the city was in near bedlam as bootleggers, gambling dens, prostitution, and bunco artists ran their businesses with little interference—provided they paid into the collective. Money flowed like booze down a drain.

With corruption rampant in City Hall and the police department, some unscrupulous officials saw opportunities to advance their political careers at the expense of others. With the public reading almost daily of payoffs, bribes, and officers being fired, citizens had become desensitized to the whole mess. However, they most certainly kept reading the articles. The public was addicted to the juicy stories the local press happily supplied—it made for good business. Topping the list were the stories of "cops and robbers" because telling the cops from the robbers was nearly impossible.

R.T. Burge, a Los Angeles police commissioner, sensed an opportunity to move up the political ladder using the day's headlines and the city's mood. Although he would not admit it, many knew he had his sights on the mayor's office. Burge was appointed to the police commission in July 1919 by the man he would soon confront, Mayor Meredith Snyder. A few months after his appointment, Burge made headlines when he charged that the LAPD was inept and crooked and that "intolerable police conditions" existed under Chief George Home's command. He alleged that several policemen had banked $50,000 to $100,000 ($650,000 to $1.3 million in today's dollars) while their official salaries were just $225 a month. Burge recommended that Chief Home step down while District Attorney Woolwine investigated the police force.

Burge missed few opportunities to spread the word of his investigation into the LAPD—even on Sundays. A superintendent of Sunday school at the Trinity Methodist Church, Burge took to the pulpit in a "special law enforcement service" and incorporated allegations of a corrupt city into his sermon. Burge accused the police force of doing nothing to end open vice in the city. Because the police force could not be trusted, he formed a personal mini-police department composed of two deputy sheriffs and a score of private detectives.

With his police department in tow, Burge obtained two warrants from the DA's office to search what he swore was a fraudulent lodging house. He led his men on a night raid of the house on West Third Street. Burge, always the self-promoter, leaked information about his raid to the press so that a large crowd, including the press, would be waiting for the show to start when the make-shift assemblage arrived. Making a grand entrance into the run-down lodging house, Burge arrested two startled individuals "for bunco" but had little or no evidence to indicate they had done anything wrong. When Burge attempted to book the "criminals," the sheriff's department and the LAPD would not participate because there wasn't enough evidence to support the allegation that a crime had been committed.

No criminal charges were ever filed on the arrests. Chief Home, perhaps to save his job, helped Burge draft civil charges against the pair for vagrancy. The defendants' attorney told the press that his clients "will be here to face the music, and somebody's going to pay the fiddler."

With no luck acting as chief of his own police force, Burge rattled the cage of District Attorney Woolwine by accusing him of failing to initiate a grand jury investigation into the LAPD for "corrupt practices." The DA commented, "No evidence upon which a grand jury investigation could be started has been presented to me by Mr. Burge. Criminal prosecutions cannot be successfully carried through on brass band methods."

Commissioner Burge ran out of targets and redirected his attention to Chief Home and his alleged failure to investigate open vice and "intolerable police conditions." Chief Home wondered to the press "why he hadn't brought any of these things to my attention," despite having had several opportunities to suggest these failures during the frequent meetings the two had. Burge answered that Home was unfit for office: "Home cannot object to a full and searching investigation of the department." Burge suggested, "If it is proven that such graft does exist, and the chief knows nothing of it, he is guilty of inefficiency. If it is proven that graft does exist among his subordinates, that he knows of it and has done nothing to eradicate it, he is guilty of neglect of duty. If either premise is proven, it will show that he is not fit to hold his office."

Home fired back, crediting the *LA Record*, not Burge, for bringing his attention to reported open gambling in the city and providing the chief with the addresses. Home commended the paper and boasted that "the gamblers have been driven out of business, bad policemen removed from the force, and operations of bunco men and pickpockets so thoroughly exposed that they are now things of the past."

Not achieving what he had hoped with the DA or the police chief, Burge went after his real target, Mayor Snyder. Through the press, Burge addressed the mayor: "Now, Mr. Mayor, there is no middle ground. You are either with me in this fight or you are with the people whom I am trying to unseat." The mayor responded, "Remarkable utterance from the Police Commissioner I appointed a few months ago. I was under the impression that his purpose was to uncover criminals in the Police Department, about which he claims to have exclusive and conclusive proof. I was not aware he was trying to unseat anyone."

The mayor brought the fight back to Burge when he issued an ultimatum: "Either submit your self-advertised corruption evidence to me at city hall or resign. There is no reason why all the men who wear the badge of a police officer of the city of Los Angeles should be made to suffer dishonor because there may be a few who have been false to a sacred trust."

When Burge provided no evidence, Mayor Snyder fired him. "The actions of Mr. Burge are demoralizing to the whole police force and, if continued, would bring about a condition of chaos."

The mayor removing Burge from his position did not alter District Attorney Woolwine's course of action. The attorney was worried about his reelection, so to keep his name on the lips of Angelenos, he pursued other leads on corruption within the LAPD. Using all resources at his disposal, including a slew of detectives, Woolwine had his men arrest a bunco man who chose to testify against his cohorts in crime rather than go to prison. The criminal reported how bunco artists and pickpockets arrived in town during the busy season, which was the winter, and had to pay certain members of the police department to receive a "license" to operate. Officers monitored these crooks by how many crime reports they received from bunco and pickpocket victims.

The *LA Record* was relentless in its attacks against the LAPD and featured headlines such as this one from April 1920: "LA LID OFF AGAIN; GAMBLING NOW OPEN." Interestingly, fired Police Commissioner Burge fed the reporters most of their information. He used his small army of private detectives to locate, name, and monitor what the police did about criminal establishments. Burge reported Chinese lottery dens as "disorderly houses and kindred places" of vice flourishing everywhere with little or no police presence. His detectives provided almost daily evidence to the *Record* to publish. The paper liked using quotes from the crooks. As one criminal said:

> You can't stop it. If you do spoil it for a while the gang will run in a new graft because there are clever rackets framed up every day. Some of the biggest fixers in the country are in town, to square the investigation and silence the parties that are making a big squawk. They've opened a sack [of money] that'll hit $50,000 to hush things up." The *Record* called the upcoming vice investigation the "biggest grand jury probe in the history of the city.

Chief Home appeared to try to counter the underworld's hold on LA. He stationed patrolmen before known gambling dens to prevent law violations and keep undesirables from entering. He ordered the law enforcement officers to make detailed reports naming those involved, to get a photograph, and to post it in police headquarters. Home set new records for arrests. Just eight months after he had taken office, the LAPD made 11,422 more arrests than during the corresponding time by the previous chief. In one four-month period ending in March 1920, 1,318 vice arrests were made. Of these, 654 were for gambling. The arrests also resulted in 54 Chinese lottery dens being shut down.

Mayor Snyder also became involved in investigating rampant vice and ordered three LA cops to be fired. These cops—and their activities—provide a glimpse into the type of crimes some on the police force committed:

- Patrolman R.H. Johnson obtained bribe money from the underworld to protect prostitutes from arrest and prosecution.
- Sergeant William Hackett was indicted twice on criminal charges alleging that he collected bribe money from the underworld.

- Patrolman Sidney Sweetnam was reported to be with a "negress" prostitute and aided in activities designed to impede an investigation by the DA's office.

With another stinging headline, "POLICE STENCH GROWS WORSE," the *Record* forced the early retirement of Chief Home: "The *Record* is forced to resume exposure of rotten, graft-ridden police conditions forced to do so by the mass of police corruption which grows worse with the passing of the weeks and months. Gambling is flourishing in LA on a hitherto unheard-of scale."

But the no-quit chief went out on his own terms. He was never indicted or charged with any crimes, and it appears he earnestly attempted to stamp out corruption within the police department. Home was overwhelmed with how corrupt the police department was. On Sept. 16, 1920, Home announced his decision to resign as chief and pursue interests in Texas with an oil company. The embattled chief was granted a one-year leave of absence and allowed to retain his previous rank of captain. However, he was unhappy with his life in Texas, so Home returned to Los Angeles and his beloved police department. He was assigned as the commanding officer of the Hollywood Division, where he was commended several times for his leadership. In 1925, Home retired for good and died in 1936.

After Chief Home resigned and moved to Texas, Mayor Snyder had a decision: whom should he choose to lead the LAPD? The answer proved so troublesome that over the next six years, two different mayors went through eight chiefs of police without finding the proper fit. On average, there was one new chief every nine months. Consequently, with no solid leadership and continual meddling from city hall, the LAPD fell to its nadir in policing the city. It did not fully recover until 1950, when Chief William H. Parker came into power.

Chapter 7

The Revolving Door of Chiefs Vice and Corruption Take Their Toll

"The mayor appoints the police commission: the police commission appoints the chief of police. Everybody who knows anything about municipal affairs knows that the mayor is the real head of the Police Department and that his word is the law."

—Los Angeles Times

The quick succession of police chiefs began anew with Lyle Pendegast (1920–1921), who was not from within the police department but was a deputy city prosecutor. As the newly appointed chief was quick to point out, what qualified him was his experience as a police executive secretary to four chiefs during the "old days" between 1905 and 1910. He knew firsthand what to expect when pinning on the chief's badge. Pendegast had a vision for the LAPD, but the tawdry city council refused most of his requests to expand the police department because they were "broke," according to the bureaucrats.

Pendegast began building the force from within. He first developed a system of personnel records for each department member. Pendegast wanted to keep track of both the officer's misdeeds and accomplishments. Using the *Daily Bulletin* to get the word to the rank and file, the chief stated that he did not want just a record of errors "but something which on the other side of the ledger gives credit to the officer who is steadily seeking to perform his duty as well as he knows how." He went so far as to issue Special Order 7: "That each officer will, after carefully considering the matter in his mind, mail to me a letter detailing briefly the circumstances of the act of official duty performed by him since January 1, 1920, which stands in his memory as the most meritorious piece of work that he has done in that time." Here was a chief of police who sincerely cared about his men and proved his devotion over and over during his short time in office. Another post on December 25, 1920, in the *Bulletin* reveals his compassion for the men: "My hearty wishes for a Merry Christmas and a happy, prosperous New Year." And then he added that he felt embarrassed "as I have not met every single officer" on the force.

Pendegast also fought to double the strength of the police force to one thousand men and asked the city to pay for the officers' uniforms. At that point, the men were required to purchase their uniforms. The chief tried to change that. But each time, the city nixed his ideas as too expensive.

As Pendegast failed in these efforts, he also found the going tough in other areas. For decades, newspapers argued that if the chief of police did not maintain a tight clamp on vice, his job tenure would be short. The newspapers only provided the proverbial key to the city to those tough, headline-grabbing vice crusaders whom the progressives loved. Pendegast understood these realities better than most as a prosecutor of vice offenders. On dozens of police raids, he led his men into back alleys, gambling dens, bordellos and then calmly ushered the offenders to jail. Even the *Record* had to stop midsentence and admit that open vice had disappeared under Pendegast's leadership.

A series of headlines overshadowed Pendegast's efforts to have an actual impact on LAPD. The headlines distracted readers, returning to the narrative of "cops and robbers." The articles had a negative effect on the morale of the LAPD.

One of these reports was the trial of Everett "Big Hutch" Hutchings, who had corrupt ties to the LAPD. Witnesses revealed that former Chief Home was a close friend of Hutchings. It was reported that in return for 17 percent of the gross, police detectives protected the crooks and allowed them to work their bunco schemes.

Indicted by the Los Angeles grand jury for grand larceny, Hutchings, the "King of Bunco," escaped to New York. Getting him back to the city turned into what one paper called the "most determined fight for the extradition of a prisoner ever waged by the district attorney's office." After wanted posters were sent nationwide, the New York Police Department notified District Attorney Woolwine that its officers had detained Hutchings. After several months, LAPD detectives finally returned Hutchings to LA. Interestingly, Hutchings arrived at the train station wearing purple goggles. Nearly the entire district attorney's office staff greeted the infamous criminal, although the big man paid them little attention.

During booking, the bunco artist started joking with arresting officers. When someone asked what his occupation was, Hutchings answered he was a "commissioner." When a reporter asked if he would testify that the LAPD was involved with his schemes, Hutchings refused to answer. He told the reporter, "Drop in again, I'll be here for a while."

As months passed and Hutchings received numerous continuances from Judge Willis, District Attorney

Woolwine boiled. Setting the stage for a future encounter with Judge Willis, Woolwine scolded the judge:

> The law's delays are calculated to foster anarchy and disrespect for constituted authority. Here is an infamous crook and scoundrel that I have sought to bring to trial for 10 months. It took about six months to drag him from the state of New York to California and after he is brought here, the courts have granted delays....For in his opinion to be wholly unjustifiable grounds....Unmerited continuances are an outrage upon the public, and an encouragement to crooks of all kinds.

Judge Willis was not happy with the confrontational DA and said so:

> It is too bad that we can't abolish courts altogether so that when the DA has a man arrested, he can be brought before the district attorney, bow three times and kneeling in humble supplication say, oh, Lord and Master give me my sentence-however you may wish it. Why not abolish courts, judges, juries and lawyers; just have the DA sentence the men when they are arrested?

During Hutchings's trial, District Attorney Woolwine and Defense Attorney Paul Schenck grew upset. The two attorneys threw insults back and forth like boxers punching it out in a heavyweight prize fight. The tension started with Schenk asking the victim, John Norris, questions. Norris allegedly was bilked out of $51,000 in a fake stock scheme. Schenck asked the victim if one of Mr. Woolwine's investigators had been staying at the victim's home. Mr. Norris said the investor had not but admitted another investigator had slept there the night before.

> Schenck: "As a matter of fact, didn't Mr. Woolwine tell you the day before yesterday at noon, that if you would come up here and testify against this man (indicating Mr. Hutchings), he would assure you that you would get your money back?"
>
> Mr. Norris: "No sir."
>
> Mr. Schenck: "Didn't he say that to you and your wife?"
>
> Mr. Woolwine: "I want an objection here Your Honor. This creature here who is accusing me of any such an infamy as that, ought to be reprimanded."
>
> Judge Willis: "Unless you have witnesses to prove that, it is a very important question."

A short discussion arose about who had informed Mr. Schenck, and he replied that he had been reliably informed.

Woolwine: "Well, you prove that, or you will account to me for it."

Schenck: "Yes, anytime."

Woolwine: "Yes, right now."

Schenck: "All right."

At this point, the court adjourned. As the judge left the chambers and the jury was filing out, Woolwine, sitting in his chair, leaned over to Schenck and cursed him. Woolwine then walked over to Schenck, seated with his legs crossed.

Woolwine: "What do you mean by asking a question like that?"

Schenck: "I have been credibly informed that the conversation I referred to took place at the DA's office."

Woolwine: "Show me the infamous liar who told you."

Schenck: "I will put him on the witness stand at the proper time."

Woolwine: "Now, tell me what you think. How do you feel about it?"

Schenck: "My personal opinion has nothing to do with it at all. That has nothing to do with it, Tom."

With that, Woolwine drew back and punched Mr. Schenck between his eyes, nearly knocking him out of his chair. Immediately, bedlam broke loose as associates for each side attempted to separate the enraged men. "You are a dirty coward to strike me while I am sitting down with my glasses on," yelled Schenck. The judge returned to the courtroom to see about the commotion. After hearing from all parties involved, Judge Willis cited Woolwine for contempt of court, arrested him for assault and battery, and made a "technical" arrest for slander and disturbing the peace. His Honor made it clear that the California Bar Association would receive a detailed report.

An LAPD officer escorted Woolwine from the court. He was booked and released on his own recognizance on all charges and was back in court by the late afternoon. In the meantime, Schenck went to the police station and obtained a concealed revolver permit. He was accompanied by the dishonorable former LAPD cop Hubert Kittle, who had earlier warned the DA to "Watch it!"

In the afternoon session, Woolwine again acted out, and the DA was once more found in contempt of court. Ultimately, Hutchings was convicted of grand larceny and ordered to serve ten years in San Quentin. It would not be the last of Big Hutch. Woolwine paid a fine and continued as the district attorney. He later played a prominent role in the investigation into the unsolved murder of movie mogul William Desmond Taylor.

As Hutchings's extraordinary trial faded from the headlines, vice again took center stage, this time by way of the mayor's office. The incumbent mayor, Meredith Snyder, was in a hotly contested election against George C. Cryer, a two-time loser in elections for city attorney and municipal judge. But Cryer's luck was about to change.

On June 1, 1921, sitting in his study at 108 West Fremont Place just a week before the election, Snyder was drawn from his work by a knock at the front door. It was getting late, but the mayor answered. A special messenger handed him a thick letter from one of his police commissioners, E. Clem Wilson, whom he had appointed one year earlier to replace fired Commissioner Burge. Mr. Wilson was the president of the Wilson & Willard Manufacturing Company and one of the city's most substantial and influential men.

Taking the letter back to his study, Mayor Snyder opened the correspondence: "Dear Sir: I hereby tender my resignation as a member of the Police Commission of the city of Los Angeles...I desire that this resignation to take effect immediately...I find myself utterly unable to continue my services under your administration." With visions of his reelection becoming blurred, the mayor read: "Among the factors is…Your failure to co-operate with the Police Commission for the best interests of the city."

Declaring that vice conditions in the city were "deplorable," Wilson charged that Snyder must have known the truth but kept the facts from the police commission for reasons no one understood. He further explained that Snyder had made a nonentity of the commission by failing to share with it police matters of vital importance to the citizens of Los Angeles. "This can mean only one of two things," Wilson went on, either Snyder "had no confidence in his police commission," or he did not want the commission to participate in handling essential matters pertaining to vice.

> Your weakening of the efficiency of the police department by unfortunate changes of personnel and policy…was forcibly emphasized recently when, either personally or through directions given to your Chief of Police, you caused a sweeping change in the vice division without, again, taking the Police Commission into your confidence….That change without the knowledge of the commission indicates that such action was exceedingly unfortunate and ill-advised.

As he ended his scathing resignation letter, Wilson accused the mayor and the chief of misleading the commission by claiming that commercialized prostitution, gambling, and other forms of vice had been "suppressed" when they truly had not. And finally, Wilson believed it was his duty "to acquaint the citizens of Los Angeles with the facts and conditions as I see them. I think the citizens are entitled to know." The following day the letter became a front-page headline in the morning *Times*.

One week later, Snyder lost to Cryer. Snider received 47 percent of the vote; Cryer received 53 percent. George Cryer became the new mayor in 1920, and there would be changes within the LAPD—there always were after an election. It was a reality in city government that the real power behind the police force came from the man sitting in the finest office in city hall. As the *Los Angeles Times* pointed out: "The mayor appoints the police commission: the police commission appoints the chief of police. Everybody who knows anything about municipal affairs knows that the mayor is the real head of the Police Department and that his word is the law." Cryer brought with him a new chief of police. Although he had tried to improve the department, Pendegast, having served for just eight months, was never allowed an honest opportunity before he was shown the door.

Mayor Cryer appointed Detective Sergeant Charles A. Jones (1921–1922) to command the police department. At the time, his appointment was considered solid political sense. Jones had twenty years on the job, and his low rank was a plus. In those corrupt days, the higher the rank, the greater the chance of advancement through political connections. Low rank meant the man owed only the mayor who appointed him.

The mayor first ordered Jones to shut down vice in the city—something that each previous chief—going back for decades—had been charged with. When the Morals Efficiency League described the disgraceful vice conditions on North Spring Street, including open gambling and abundant prostitution and liquor, the newspapers ran with it. The stories, which dominated the press, pointed out that gambling kingpins had arranged the transfer of the Central Division police commander because he actively enforced the anti-vice statutes. With the mayor's approval, the captain was replaced with the vice lords' hand-picked man.

Despite his best efforts, Jones was criticized for not shutting down vice in the city. Chief Jones angrily replied: "No one can run the Los Angeles Police Department. There are too many meddlesome so-called reformers and others who interfere. The job isn't worth the grief that attends to it." After just six months, the detective sergeant turned chief was out, opting for an early retirement. As he walked out of his office for the last time, a police reporter witnessed him throw his thumb over his shoulder and point at the office of the chief of police. He said, "When they decide to get you, they get you."

After just a few months in office, the mayor was again ready to name a new chief of police. In an insightful quote, Cryer shifted the blame for the rotating door in the chief's office from his office to the very citizens who elected him:

> The police department has been a storm center for many years past. With few exceptions, one police regime after another has crumbled and fallen. Honest heads of the department have failed to receive the coordinated support of our best citizens. Avalanche after avalanche of criticism and attack after attack have been visited upon the department. Some have been just, but many have been unjust. The whole has served to weaken and disrupt the morale of the department. Instead of encouraging the department with words of commendation for deeds accomplished, many citizens have made it a practice to go up and down the street announcing that "the morale of our police department is all shot to pieces."

As chiefs of police came and went in quick secession, almost none had fought back against the political interference that eventually caused their demise. Not so for the next chief. Mayor Cryer appointed retired Army Colonel James W. Everington (1922), a shoot-from-the-hip, battle-scarred veteran from the Great War, to take charge of the LAPD. No one seemed to care that he had no police background. The *Record* led the Everington bandwagon by describing the appointment as a "miracle" that would introduce a "new era of clean government." In taking office, the Army colonel announced, "I want to get into the saddle before I state what I am going to do." And then, as if predicting the shortest term for a appointed chief in the LAPD's history, Everington said, "I realize I will be unable to please everybody." Never has the LAPD police department had a more boisterous chief of police (except perhaps Daryl Gates in the 1980s.)

With Colonel Everington, the police department was getting an outspoken veteran who could have listed "courageous" on his resume. As one of his peers said: "The bravest man, with the exception of one, I have ever known." The soldier, who fought beside the colonel, said, "The other man is dead."

Upon taking office, Chief Everington declared to the city and his police force that his number one priority was cleaning up LA by eliminating vice. Everington announced in the police *Bulletin*:

> The people believe that the recent order to 'Clean Up' is the usual bluff of a new chief. It is not. If anyone of any rank tells you to 'stay off' of any one or any place, or to drop any "lead" you are following, accept the order or tip, and pretend you are going to obey it. Then come directly to me.

Just two months later, the chief said he was disappointed in the results of his changes to the department's culture. To emphasize his point, he suspended two high-ranking officers: W.L. Spellman, the captain of Central Division, and Lieutenant A.W. Gifford, who oversaw the vice squad. Everington called the two men into his office and informed them that their results had not met the instructions he had given his first day. Consequently, they were relieved of duty. In essence, he fired them.

In a statement to the press defending his position, the chief went straight to the point:

> When I came into office, I gave orders to clean up the city. I am sorry to say that Los Angeles is just as wide open today as it was when I issued those instructions. My

instructions were not carried out. As long as I remain in office, I am going to be Chief of Police and this city will know it twenty years later.

Everington grasped that almost every chief before him had had the same plan. He believed the trouble was that "when they attempted to carry them out, they were removed or were called off." No way was this going to happen to Everington.

Some business elite, who did not want vice closed, fought against him. They especially wanted prostitution and gambling to remain, as both were good for business. Consequently, almost from the start of his administration, there was a movement to remove the chief.

In another interview with the press, Everington said, "Crookedness exists in the police department." When the Civil Service Commission was about to appoint the two highest positions under the chief, Everington said no. "If civil service men get those two positions, then I, as head of the department, would not have the power to fire them or transfer them…if they failed to make good." To weed out this corruption, he needed his own hand-picked men at the top levels of his command. According to his boss, the mayor, the man to be placed as his first assistant chief, did not have a clue. A high-ranking officer told Everington, "I don't know where they get this bunk about graft in the department." In all his years on the job, the officer said, he had never known of any instances of graft.

"Reports showed me that the underworld was running without interruption," the chief said. "I obtained proof that there was crookedness in the department and referred them to my assistant for verification. The report was a coat of whitewash for the suspected one." Everington went against civil service regulations, demoted the man to captain, and transferred him to an outlying substation. In frustration, the chief admitted, "It is not possible for an honest man to be chief of police."

Mayor Cryer, who had appointed Everington, continued to support the chief, despite a growing chorus to fire him. The mayor condemned the bankers, landlords, and vice entrepreneurs for exerting "insidious pressure" to undermine Everington. The mayor said he would support his chief "to the fullest extent possible."

At least two police judges also undermined the police department, according to John Pelletier of the Morals Efficiency League. These were the same two judges whom former Chief Jones had singled out. The two judges operated their courtroom by working with a select group of attorneys who handled vice cases. The judges routinely freed prostitutes these attorneys defended and convicted women other attorneys represented. Working behind the scenes, Pelletier discovered evidence of a group of LAPD officers who warned the targets of police raids usually a day in advance.

On April 12, 1922, the police commission hearings began for the two vice supervisors Everington had fired, Captain Spellman and Lieutenant Gifford. The resulting testimony gave an insider's look at protected vice practices in Los Angeles. A procession of witnesses supported the two fired men. Their testimony supported the officers and suggested they were who the "underworld feared most." The defense attorney for the two dismissed officers pointed an accusatory finger at Everington, accusing the chief of "mishandling" the LAPD and his two clients. The lawyer supported his argument with statistics that he threw out like seeds on a new lawn. Burglaries for March had risen to twice the number they had been the previous year. Homicides were up over 500 percent. Others testified that vice was still as prevalent as before Everington had taken command; criminals were being more careful to avoid detection. Even the district attorney's office jumped on the anti-Everington bandwagon, claiming that the chief had created a false issue.

The hard-nosed Everington, who had fought in World War I and now in the streets of Los Angeles, would not go down without a fight. He returned to the trenches and attacked anyone who did not appear to support him. He blamed the police commission, especially De La Monte. He accused the city prosecutor of not properly cross-examining questionable witnesses. When Mayor Cryer adjourned the hearings for the weekend, Everington suggested that the recess was intended to thwart him. When the case did resume the following week, a fuming Cryer refused to confirm the chief had his support.

The most damaging testimony against Everington came from within the LAPD's ranks. A very senior captain testified that a policeman must "play policy. I do myself. If I didn't, I would have to look for another job." The captain testified that the LAPD was disorganized and that every policeman was more concerned about protecting his job than enforcing the law. He further said that vice could not be eliminated because the powers that profited from vice would not allow it. The captain also explained that criminal leaders and profiteers would do whatever it took to keep the money machine running. Most of these criminals and profiteers, he said, were in city government. But an intractable captain who would not cooperate with the criminal element could quickly be silenced. "Bookmakers told me if I didn't quit arresting them, I would be transferred. Chief Jones transferred me the next day. He didn't tell me why, and I didn't ask."

The overwhelming testimony against Everington left the mayor wordless and embarrassed. The police commission ruled that the chief had not substantiated his charge that the men were derelict in their duties and restored both officers to the force with back pay.

Everington responded as if he had been the one on trial, attacking all those he determined were out to get him. Throwing the mayor in with the police commissioners, he said they were all "spineless jellyfish" and "weak kneed creatures of expediency." He described the reformers who brought him to the forefront to be the chief of police as "the soft-heads and saps who have showered me with resolutions…I have told them all to go to hell."

With the police department in turmoil and almost all in city government agreeing that the chief needed to move on, people began shouting for his dismissal. But the stubborn chief would not quite or allow himself to be fired, claiming he was "framed" and "gotten," that he was being "forced out." Instead of leaving town, the tenacious chief issued an ultimatum to the citizens of Los Angeles. If the community truly wanted reform, they had ten days to come forward and prove it. The citizens never got the opportunity as Mayor Cryer removed Everington from office on April 20, 1922. His term—which lasted four months—was the shortest term for an appointed chief in the LAPD's history.

The reason Everington failed as a leader might have been, as the *Times* pointed out, because "the chief did not realize the philosophy of going quietly to work to learn his new job and to execute its duties, without so much excitement…without so many accusations that his supporters were deserting him." Or perhaps no one could clean up LA. As the *Times* wrote in an editorial:

> To actually and permanently "clean up" a city the size of Los Angeles is, of course, impossible; it never has been done and it never can be done. Like jimson weeds and fleas, all that can be done with law-breakers is to keep hoeing and scratching and keep the crop down to the minimum of activity. The more elbow grease and the less oratory used the more results achieved.

The next chief of police would take the *Times* article to heart. Mayor Cryer went with an insider when he appointed Detective Sergeant Louis D. Oaks (1922–1923) to lead the department. Born in Missouri in 1882, Oaks moved to Los Angeles in 1910 and soon after joined the LAPD. He had been a detective for twelve years and flew under the radar. He performed his assignments in an exemplary way, never seeking notoriety. The tall, good-looking man lived quietly with his wife and daughter and went about his career unspectacularly, which appealed to Cryer. With the vocal support of the rank and file, who were delighted to rid themselves of Colonel Everington, the police department was ready to move forward under Oaks. Or so everyone thought.

Cryer soon let slip why he had appointed such a low-ranking officer as chief of police. He understood that a sergeant was used to taking orders, and this was precisely the kind of man he wanted running the LAPD. Like a puppet on strings, the mayor hoped to control the chief's every movement. To the press, the mayor exclaimed that the days of "no strings" attached from the mayor's office to the police department were over. Interestingly, while that sounded like tough talk, a force in the background directed the mayor. Kent Kane Parrot was the puppeteer calling the shots.

Parrot was a handsome man with a boyish grin and magnetism. He was also adept at getting two diametrically opposed personalities into a room and, in short order, having them become friends. In the corrupt days of the 1920s, Parrot was a natural.

A star football player at the University of Southern California, Parrot graduated with a law degree and was immediately admitted to the bar. Understanding that he could become rich if he controlled the mayor, Parrot searched for the right "yes man" to get elected. In 1921, Parrot decided George Cryer, an assistant district attorney who had run for political office twice and lost, was the perfect person to run for mayor. Parrot acted as his campaign manager.

The plan to get Cryer elected was simple—tell the voters exactly what they wanted to hear. So, the Parrot team promised every Protestant minister, every progressive, every temperance consortium, and every anti-vice crusader that they would again put LA on the path to greatness by eliminating all vice. The reformers loved it. With the support of the progressives, the vice syndicate was confident that Mayor Cryer was the man for the job and helped get him elected. After Cryer took office, he kept his promise to protect the vice lords from the police.

Profiting most from Parrot's mingling were men like Charlie Crawford, who owned the Maple Bar, an upscale watering hole with an elegant bordello upstairs. His customers were the elite of Los Angeles. They included politicians, judges, city officials, and the business elite who enjoyed the finer things in life. They all loved Charlie and his booze, but especially his prostitutes. Crawford had the support of the criminal elite like Albert Marco, a gangster who ran the city's prostitution ring, a gambler, and former LAPD vice detective, Guy McAfee, who was fired for running a gambling operation out of a police station. And most of the LA criminals who wanted to improve their well-being. For this privileged group, vice was not a racket but a business.

To ensure that competition was kept in its place, the collective needed an enforcer. LAPD Lieutenant Dick Lucas was just that soldier. He once was described as "a racketeer with a gun buttressed by the authority of a police badge." Lucas was a big man: over six feet tall and weighed 250 pounds. The Thomson sub-machine gun he always had nearby made him even more intimidating. When gangsters from back East envisioned fresh pickings in sunny Los Angeles, they sent their lieutenants to check out the turf. On most occasions, Lucas met them and sent them packing with the warning that they would find themselves on a slab in the local morgue if they returned.

When Chicago gangster Al "Scarface" Capone visited Los Angles, detectives Lucas and Lieutenant "Roughhouse" Brown met his entourage and trailed Capone for three days. Capone said he was just a tourist with a lot of money to spend and did not think it was fair that the LA police were telling him to get out of town. "This is a fine thing to happen to me. I never was run out of anywhere before. I only wanted a rest from business." Escorted to the railroad station by the LAPD, Capone and his men were sent home. The press gave the story an appropriate headline: "Scarface Al—Came to Play, Now Look—He's Gone Away!"

Not going away was the city council, which began making a ruckus soon after Oaks became chief. Leading the negative publicity against the LAPD was the council president, Ralph L. Criswell, who had set his sights on being elected to the U.S. Congress. According to the *Times*, Criswell "stood the City Hall on its ear" when he declared that commercialized gambling was netting $25,000 a night, and 60 percent of that money was spent on hush money— bribes. Addressing the assembled council and press, he declared that the city's vice conditions were "worse than ever before." He asserted that LA was the "mecca" for gamblers from around the country because "the going is good. I know what I am talking about, and I could tell you much more."

Chief Oaks responded by arguing that gambling and other forms of vice were "at low ebb," and conditions were steadily improving. The usually taciturn Oaks then ramped it up: "I am sick and tired of the attitude of Councilman Criswell. He has started something with me, and I am going to finish it! I do not intend to sit back and allow him to make such accusations as he has without fighting back. Councilman Criswell has either got to put up or shut up." Chief Oaks told the press that the attack on the police department was without foundation and that Criswell was using his position for "political advertising."

Mayor Cryer joined in. He criticized the council president for not taking the matter up with the police commission, the chief, or himself, even though, according to the mayor, Criswell had had several opportunities. "I think Criswell made a mistake in shouting the matter from the housetops."

Making headlines almost daily, Criswell kept the pressure up. He described where vice was rampant and said the LAPD was standing by and allowing it to happen while receiving kickbacks. As the weeks passed, Criswell continued his relentless attacks; his council colleagues began to disagree and distance themselves from him. They voiced their support for the police department. Councilman William Mushet said Chief Oaks was among the best Los Angeles chiefs ever. He said Oaks had not been appointed chief for political reasons, which he offered as praise. Another councilman, Robert Sparks, also came to Oaks's side. "We have become so accustomed to the periodical abuse of the Police Department by President Criswell that the novelty has worn off, and it is tiresome." The mayor added his support for the department: "It's the same old story. Also, the same old charges were investigated by the grand jury and dismissed." He said the LAPD "is vigorously prosecuting law violators" and that crime conditions compared favorably with those in similarly sized cities. With all this support, Criswell's allegations quickly faded from the news.

Meeting behind closed doors in smoke-filled rooms, some of the most powerful men in Los Angeles announced that all the infighting concerning the LAPD must stop. They believed a clean city with little or no vice and corruption was best for the city and, thus their wallets. With leadership from the *Times* and the *Examiner*, the Community Development Association was formed. The CDA's directors included the presidents of a large life insurance company, a major oil company, the state labor council, and a member of the banking community. Also included in the general membership were representatives from some of the city's most prestigious organizations. This included the Men's City Club, the Women's City Club, and all five major newspapers.

Crime skyrocketed over 300 percent between 1919 and 1923, partly due to a 42 percent increase in the population. The CDA wanted to ensure that the police department and the courts would function at their "maximum efficiency." To accomplish this, they formed the Anti-Crime Commission. One of its first efforts was to team up with Chief of Police Oaks to get more officers on the street and, importantly, to get these men a salary increase. The argument was simple. How could the city expect to enroll high-caliber men for police service when the men were offered pay on a par with ditch diggers and garbage collectors?

The commission argued that it was no wonder so many "incompetents" and "crooks" had found their way into the police ranks. mThey reasoned that many could not resist the criminal underworld's bribes and kickbacks because they received minimal pay. The Anti-Crime Commission understood that if you cleaned up the police department, you cleaned up the city. Listening to these suggestions, the city council increased personnel by 40 percent and raised salaries by 20 percent.

Despite the CDA's support, the LAPD continued to flounder. Different entities took turns disparaging the police and Chief Oaks. Kent Parrot, the man who single-handedly got Mayor Cryer elected, led the disruption. Parrot, a leading underworld figure, aligned himself with everyone from bootleggers and vice lords to elected officials. Every significant decision in the city went through Parrot. Becoming more confident, Parrot tightened his control on police headquarters. Parrot, a civilian who had no elected position, bribed vice supervisors and assigned bagmen to handle payoffs. He transferred officers to better serve his criminal activities without consulting the police chief. Kent Parrot's word was law because he owned the law.

Meanwhile, Chief Louis Oaks did not sit back ideally but continually fought Parrot for control of the LAPD. It was a battle of a nearly powerless public official against an entrenched corrupt hoodlum. When Oaks continued to try to run the police force his way, Parrot ordered Oaks to his plush new apartment at the Biltmore Hotel to discuss policy and issue orders. Mayor Cryer ordered the chief to attend. Oaks refused. Maneuvering around the chief like he did not exist, Parrot dealt with the chief's subordinates, who knew that if they did not follow Parrot's orders, they would be quickly transferred or fired. The manager of the Harbor Commission, Charles E. Richards, substantiated this type of outside interference. He complained publicly that "Mr. Parrot's sinister shadow" was constantly meddling in commission business to the point that Richards lost control of his commission and resigned in frustration.

While many of Chief Oaks's supporters fought Parrot's influence over the LAPD, others took advantage of the political boost Parrot's power offered in terms of promotions and special attention. One who took such advantage was R. Lee Heath, captain of Central Division and previous interim chief of police. When the police commission questioned Captain Heath, he admitted that he disobeyed orders when it suited him and suppressed evidence when necessary. He was perhaps overly confident with these comments because he had Parrot in his corner. As captain of Central Division, Heath said he moved around key vice personnel to serve the mayor's needs. These actions, along with the mayor's control over the police department, made headlines after Chief Oaks fired Captain Heath in July 1923.

In a lengthy, comprehensive affidavit, Oaks itemized the numerous offenses leading to Heath's firing. Heading the list was Heath's "attitude" toward Chief Oaks, who described the captain as "very curt, defiant, disrespectful and insubordinate." Heath disobeyed direct orders and failed to investigate reported vice conditions in his division, Oaks said. He transferred men to the vice division without permission and put a sergeant indicted for bribery in charge of vice operations. Additionally, Heath was accused of participating in politics in violation of department regulations. The chief provided examples. During a campaign, Heath prepared a "Police-Fire Department Slate" of candidates and attempted to assign members of both departments to hang political posters—while on duty. When Chief Oaks attempted to transfer Heath from Central Division because he allegedly protected vice activities, Mayor Cryer intervened and ordered the chief to keep Heath and his vice squad intact.

To ensure people adhered to his orders, the mayor assigned his secretary, H.H. Kinney, to spy on Chief Oaks. The chief added that to his affidavit. He documented how Kinney forced him to transfer people to the central vice unit even though the chief knew these transfers were improper as the officers were known vice supporters.

Kinney flaunted his control over the chief, even referring to himself in the third person: "No one had better question Kinney's honesty. When they do, Kinney will strike back, and when he strikes, he will strike first." Kinney further embarrassed Oaks when he took the chief's new department Cadillac for his personal use.

When Oaks did discipline Heath, the chief reported that Parrot protested. In a phone call to the chief, Parrot demanded, "What the hell is the matter with you, anyhow?" Oaks angrily retorted, "Neither you nor anyone else is going to use the Police Department for political purposes."

Heath's dismissal by the chief was set for a hearing before the police commission on August 2. Yet on August 1, the chief of police—who openly fought City Hall politics and Kent Parrot—was unceremoniously fired. Mayor Cryer said the official reason was the police had discovered Oaks in his car with a young woman and a bottle of bootleg whiskey, thereby violating several laws. Removing Chief Oaks from the picture, Cryer, over the objection of at least one police commissioner, reinstated Heath to his old rank of captain. Heath was told to stay out of politics—a slap on the wrist. All of Chief Oaks's documented charges against Heath were dismissed.

The political-criminal combination in Los Angeles functioned much more efficiently when they could control the police chief. They also understood that repeatedly removing chiefs shattered police morale and effectiveness and emboldened the progressive constituency by putting police reform back in the headlines. Consequently, the criminal syndicate understood that, at times, putting a reform-minded chief in office was necessary. This cycle of reform and corruption was a hallmark of LA politics for decades. With the removal of Oaks, the combination, through Mayor Cryer, named August Vollmer, the famed criminologist and police scientist, as the new LAPD chief of police. Not since Chief Glass of the 1890s had the police department had such a leader capable of taking the force to the next level of proficiency. It would be the calm before the storm.

Chapter 8

The Man from Berkeley

"No group of pin-headed politicians nor the press will run this department while I am here."

—August Vollmer, Chief of Police

The LAPD's Harbor Division was located a long way from City Hall. Some officers believed they would be walking a beat on the piers in San Pedro if they did not behave. But the new chief, August Vollmer, just used the venue to state how things would now be different. With the entire division gathered around him at the port, the chief of police, on leave from Berkeley Police Department in California, announced that the LAPD would run on its own merits. "No group of pin-headed politicians nor the press will run this department while I am here."

> The newspapers have over-advertised me in all but one thing. They did not mention that outside interests will no longer run this department or sandbag its officers. The trouble here, as in the past, has been that they have given you a saw and hammer and expected you to build a Biltmore Hotel. You need more money and

facilities, and I am going to do my best to get them for you.

A spontaneous cheer went up from the gathered troops. Vollmer had their attention.

I want to sell you to the people of Los Angeles, the press and the pulpit. I want to promise you that these pin-headed politicians, these queer guys, will no longer sandbag you. You have been sandbagged...for so many years that it has ruined your morale.

Vollmer took his message to the community through the Trinity M. E. Church a few days later. The politically active Reverend R.P. Schuler had invited him. Vollmer delivered his message of faith—that the LAPD could be turned around.

The police department is shot to pieces, by the attacks that have been made on it. But whether I stay or not, it will be saved, if a good, honest man is kept at the head and you support him. The question is do the people of Los Angeles really want the city cleaned up or do they only want it veneered? If you want it cleaned up, I will stay with you. It is not the Los Angeles Chief of Police you want to back up but the Los Angeles Police Department. If one man in the department goes wrong, don't blame the department; its members are only human.

Taking the stage after Vollmer, Marshal Stimpson, president of the Southern California Civil Service League, said: "Whenever any mayor or mayor's secretary or police commission interferes with the program of Chief Vollmer, I hope that the people of Los Angeles will politely say to that official, 'Here's your hat, what's your hurry—good-by.'"

As Vollmer talked, and he traveled and talked a lot, people began to listen. Many asked who he was. In 1888, the Vollmer family moved from New Orleans to San Francisco and, soon after that, to Berkeley. When he was nineteen, Vollmer opened a coal and feed store and quickly moved on to organize the Berkeley volunteer fire department. When the United States went to war against Spain, Vollmer enlisted in the Army and fought against guerrilla forces in the Philippines. Returning to Berkeley as a decorated combat veteran, Vollmer worked as a mail carrier. Vollmer had an athletic build and a natural ability to lead. Soon the *Berkeley Daily Gazette* discovered him and suggested he run for city marshal. He agreed and won handily. Later, the marshal's office was dissolved into the Berkeley Police Department, with Vollmer as its chief. In a short time, Vollmer became known worldwide for his theories of scientific policing, which included modern technology, training officers, and professionalizing police standards.

Toward the end of Chief Oaks's career, the Los Angeles Crime Commission searched for the next chief. The commission sent a survey to the leading chiefs of police across the country and discovered that one name kept appearing, Chief Vollmer of Berkeley. After thoroughly examining Vollmer's methods and his successful results, the Crime Commission invited Vollmer for an interview. They wanted to discuss the police problems in Los Angeles and how he would manage them. If they liked his answers, the commissioners would offer him the job.

Chief Vollmer listened intently to what the commissioners presented. He made his suggestions, and the commission liked what they heard. They offered him the job. Before accepting, Vollmer made one significant stipulation. He would come to Los Angeles as the next chief of the LAPD, provided he would not have to battle politicians or political pressures within or outside the department. Vollmer wanted to be left alone to devote himself to policing the city and professionalizing the police force.

The commission agreed and went to Mayor Cryer to inform him of Vollmer's conditions. The mayor agreed he would do everything he could to shield Vollmer from the outside political influences that were constantly attempting to control the police force. When everyone agreed, Vollmer said he would take a one-year leave of absence from Berkeley beginning August 1, 1923, to test his theories and hopefully improve the LAPD.

In an article for the *Los Angeles Times* titled "Prestige and the Police," Alma Whitaker captured the essence of the LAPD's newest chief.

> He is a curious and unique character, this new Chief of ours. Tall, spare, gray, alert, courageous, he just oozes psychologic theories, analytic etiology, scientific experimentation, tabulated information, and he loves charts, maps, statistics, blue prints, indexes, records, figures. Everything he says or does is worked out on a chronological basis. He loves to make little drawings to illustrate his points. And he loves to talk, to explain, to propound, convince and marshal evidence.

Not since Chief Glass in the 1890s had the LAPD found a leader capable of taking the force to the next level of professionalism. Vollmer was one of the most respected names in law enforcement. Besides being the celebrated Berkeley chief of police, Vollmer founded the School of Criminology at the University of California, Berkeley, where he often lectured. Vollmer's methodical philosophy was radical in an era of tough cops who had a "hit first" mentality and were quick to use their guns and batons.

Chief Vollmer advanced two crucial fundamentals to professionalize the LAPD and reform the city. First, there needed to be a competent police force without political interference. It needed to be comprised of intelligent, highly trained, well-paid officers who used the latest technology. Second, there needed to be a supportive citizenry that understood crime was a community problem. Citizens, to combat it, had to hold an active sentiment against crime and criminals. The community must know that these commitments came with a price and would accept the accompanying taxation. Vollmer asked that the law-abiding citizens resolve never to berate, belittle, or bribe police officers.

Vollmer criticized Hollywood and the media. He detested ludicrous film portrayals of policemen, such as the Keystone Kops. He feared impressionistic kids would grow up watching such frivolity and believe what they saw even as they matured into adults. These pictures depicted policemen as idiots and crooks. Vollmer demanded that motion picture producers, writers, reporters, and others with influence "cease to describe the police as numbskulls" and stop glorifying the criminals. Remarkably, many agreed.

Vollmer understood the importance of talking to service clubs, church associations, and other groups that would listen. He wanted to organize cooperation and support for the police department. During his lectures, Vollmer pointed out the 12 percent rule: 12 percent of society enthusiastically upheld the law while 12 percent broke the law. Therefore, supporters must organize to battle crime alongside the police. This battle did not involve physical acts, but choosing problems in the community supporters felt were important. These problems might include juvenile delinquents in the neighborhood, burglaries, or probation issues. The chief suggested that supporters investigate issues thoroughly and suggest reforms. Finally, supporters should monitor the performance of public officials to confirm that the new standards were being upheld.

The new chief convinced City Hall to hire an additional 250 police officers, many of whom were housed in one of the five newly commissioned stations. Vollmer established a police school to train these officers, the first extensive school of its kind. The training lasted ninety days and would one day become the LAPD Police Academy a decade later. The school taught all aspects of law enforcement. Vollmer developed a relationship with the University of Southern California for additional training. He stressed the importance of courtesy and appearance and cooperating with community organizations such as churches and service clubs. With all the new feet on the ground, the chief also fought for and won the addition of sixty-three police cars and sixty motorcycles to the department's growing fleet.

The chief argued for higher salaries, "How can you expect to get intelligent men for $120 a month when they can make $165 driving a milk wagon?" The citizens of Los Angeles agreed. Salaries gradually increased from $100 to $120 monthly to $140 to $170.

Vollmer addressed other pressing issues as well. He focused on the incessant problem of vice and police payoffs since these issues continually made headlines and demoralized the department. The community members who read these vice stories lost respect for the police force, and department morale suffered accordingly. It was an endless and brutal cycle that never fully allowed for the enhancement of the department. In a bold move, Vollmer made vice abatement a separate agency from the police department, which had separate commanders. By segregating vice abatement and the associated corruption, the police department could sidestep the ramifications of vice.

Vollmer often talked about the distinction between vice and crime. Like many large cities, he thought it wrong that Los Angeles regarded the suppression of vice as more important than crime. As Vollmer pointed out, in countries where gambling was not illegal and vice was considered a public health question, the police could function with infinitely more honor and success.

Vollmer listed fighting crime as a top priority. He filled all the divisions with maps and charts on which every robbery, every burglary, and every stolen automobile was carefully marked. Vollmer used small colored pins that told at a glance where most of the offenses had been committed, the time of the day they had been committed, and the type of crime. With this documentation, Chief Vollmer formed an "Invisible Squad," or the "Crime Crushers," as they became known, with top-performing officers. This new division was the forerunner of today's Metropolitan Division, which consisted of three hundred men and nine captains. Vollmer tasked this highly mobile force with cleaning up "nests" of crime. Vagrants, gambling houses, vice locations, and bootleggers were the new focus. Using new faster cars and motorcycles, the plainclothes officers could respond to any "hot spot" in the city. Vollmer believed that by breaking up the criminal gangs and keeping them on the move, the Crime

Crushers would prevent many burglaries and robberies. Vollmer elaborated, "We are going to use this force for surgical operations. There are several crime ulcers in the city and the Invisible Division will cut them out. Nobody will know anything about the movements of the division except the chief of police and the commanding officer of the division."

The chief warned the organized criminals of Los Angeles that "many would die" in his attack on crime. He issued a standing order: "Shoot to kill." Vollmer directed his force to respond to areas with higher crime numbers. The Crime Crushers' effectiveness was immediate. Auto thefts went from an average of twenty-five per day to six. The Crime Crushers arrested fifty-six burglars and thirty robbers within a month. Six career criminals were killed in highly publicized gun battles with the squad. The Crime Crushers were a monumental success.

But not everything went according to plan. As in the past, the powerful police commission became a hindrance, blocking many of the chief's efforts to clean up the department. In October, the Crime Commission issued a rebuke to commissioners Charles H. De Coo and John H. De La Monte (the mayor was the third commissioner) for failing to support the chief as they had promised. Things came to a head when Vollmer fired two patrolmen for extortion. When they appeared before the police commission for their hearing, Commissioners De Coo and De La Monte reinstated the men on a technicality. When Vollmer produced additional evidence of the patrolmen's guilt, the commissioners ruled that the case was closed and could not be reopened.

Speaking before the City Club, Vollmer described the lack of support he saw:

> In spite of everything that can be done, irresponsible and crooked men sometimes manage to worm their way into the police department, but this condition can be remedied by getting the right type of men on the Police Commission so that when the chief makes an honest effort to get rid of the rats, crooks and lazy bones he will be supported. The hole through which men may enter the police department as officers should be made as small as possible, but the hole through which they may be ejected should be made as wide as all out-of-doors.

Both commissioners were mentioned in several other controversies, and some of their actions appeared to be illegal. Consequently, Mayor Cryer dismissed De La Monte, after which De Coo resigned. On his way out, De La Monte declared that Vollmer would not last and Captain R.L. Heath would be appointed chief. But Heath surprised many when he stated he did not want the job and considered Vollmer, the country's top policeman. However, that stance did not last long.

Vollmer's attempt to keep himself isolated from the politicians became increasingly difficult. While the Crime Commission initially succeeded in keeping the politicians at bay, the commission could not sustain this. Vollmer expected the Crime Commission to protect the department against outside influences, but his hope was unrealistic. It all came down to perceptions. Many viewed Vollmer as a tool of the Crime Commission, believing that the commission was simply one more political machine contending for control of the city. District Attorney Asa Keyes called out the commission in a published statement. He wrote that he was "sick and tired of the commissions implied intimidation." He continued: "They [the Crime Commission] have furnished me with a mass of hearsay and intangible evidence aimed in nearly every instance against the proponents of municipal ownership." By separating himself from the commission, Keys wanted to drive a wedge between the Crime Commission, which supported Chief Vollmer, and the public to weaken the chief's position.

The commission was quick to reply. In a public statement, the commission berated the district attorney for issuing such falsehoods. "It is apparent" that Keyes was out to mislead the public. The commission reminded the community that it existed "solely to secure greater safety for the lives and property of the citizens of this community. It is not concerned in any way with politics or political issues."

The commissioners asked the DA if he was upset because "in the performance of their duties, they have been compelled to call to the notice of the district attorney frequently and forcefully what the commission conceived to be the most flagrant shortcomings and delinquencies in the conduct of his office."

Case in point: when Keyes was in the process of secretly securing the release of Everett A. "Big Hutch" Hutchings on parole, which the commission labeled "as a ringleader of bunco and one of the most notorious criminals in the country," the commission stepped in as the representatives for Los Angeles's citizens to stop it.

Political implications aside, the city council was becoming concerned with the rising cost of police service. From 1920 to 1925, department employees rose from 732 to 2,364. Salaries were significantly increased, which put financial stress on the city coffers. The annual budget grew from $1.3 million in 1921 to nearly $4 million in 1924. The once supportive city council soon became intractable and did an about-face denying projects the chief introduced. When Vollmer told the chief jailer to purchase clocks for the jail for $100, the council told the jailer to go to a second-hand store and buy $5 worth of alarm clocks rather "than burden the taxpayers with such absurd cost."

The struggle in council chambers, the political instability, the mayor, the DA, and constant headlines about crime and vice began to take their toll on the chief. One observer noted Vollmer as being "tired, jaded, his voice nervously sharp." The chief reminded the politicians and his supporters that he had only agreed to one year. While attending a luncheon with his friends on June 30, 1924, Vollmer announced his upcoming departure. A week later, he formally notified the mayor. As he was closing out his year in office, Vollmer said that reforming the inner workings of the police department had been more difficult than he had expected. He said the job was more than he could handle. As the exit light grew brighter, Vollmer could take pride in LAPD's impact in lowering crime. Burglary arrests were up by 90 percent over the previous year; robbery arrests were up 182 percent; felony arrests were up 19 percent, and misdemeanor arrests were up 30 percent. Despite the population increasing by 12 percent, the rate per capita for "hard" crimes had been reduced by 10 percent over the previous year. Open vice had been pushed to the city's fringes. For the most part, vice was out of sight and no longer significant in daily life as in previous years.

By any standard, Chief Vollmer had accomplished much. In just one year, he had added over eight hundred officers to the force; established a ninety-day police academy to train them; added five new police stations; and demonstrated the necessity of statistics and daily crime reporting. He had instilled in the police force the importance of courtesy, appearance, and positive community relations. He had added scores of new vehicles and motorcycles, had the entire department take the U.S. Army's Alpha Intelligence Test to better assign personnel, and expanded the fingerprint bureau from two to nineteen.

No other chief in the first half of the twentieth century had had a more significant impact than August Vollmer. But most importantly, Vollmer had provided the framework for future generations, demonstrating that when the chief of police was under civil service protection, a group of honest policemen could defeat organized criminals. His reforms moved the LAPD toward professionalization earlier than most big-city police departments. While corruption was always on the police force's periphery, Vollmer positively influenced such up-and-coming future chiefs as James E. Davis and, later, William H. Parker. These two men would take the department to even greater heights of excellence. These leaders were handed the sword of professionalism that the LAPD would use in their endless battle against corruption and political interference.

In an editorial titled "The Gathering Vultures," the *Los Angeles Times* scanned the heavens and saw evil descending from the skies of corruption. The vultures were gathering, the paper warned, now that Vollmer was taking his reforms and ingenuity back to Berkeley:

> The ravenous horde of big and little gamblers, bunko men, "campaign fund" collectors, pimps, bootleggers, drug peddlers and crooks of every other description are already dealing in "concessions," earnestly hopeful that…they will see a return to the halcyon days when the town was wide open, the police were in politics and anything went.

The *Times* felt strongly that Vollmer "showed Los Angeles for the first time that it is possible to run its police department as a police department and nothing else; that it is possible to tell the political bosses of the administration in plain language where they can go; that an honest chief with bowels and backbone and brains need to have no fear of the yapping jackals as his heels."

As politicians and crooks, the vultures were confident in their return to power. As Vollmer left office on September 1, billboards across the city announced who was now in charge when they proclaimed: "THE FIRST OF SEPTEMBER WILL BE THE LAST OF AUGUST."

With Vollmer gone, many politicians in City Hall did not believe in lessons learned; they wanted a return to the status quo—a return to politicizing the LAPD. Vollmer's replacement, R.L. Heath, did not disagree with them.

Chapter 9

Gangsters, Prohibition, Corruption, and the Nadir of the LAPD

"Conditions are normal. There is bound to be vice, but so far as organized vice is concerned or any police protection for vice, there is nothing of that sort in Los Angeles."

—R. Lee Heath, Chief of Police

Assistant Captain of Detectives Taylor was busy at his desk at police headquarters trying to get caught up on paperwork. As he worked, he caught a glimpse of two people approaching his desk. It took only a second for him to recognize one of them as Milton "Farmer" Page, LA's flamboyant, picturesque gambling king. The other was Page's attorney, Warren Williams. As they approached the desk, Page calmly said, "Hello." Then exclaimed, "I'm the man who killed Joseph, but I did it in self-defense." The entire floor of LAPD's finest detectives halted what they were doing to see what the underworld kingpin was up to. The other assistant captain of detectives, Bean, who was handling the case of the fatal shooting, which had happened the day before, took Page into custody and hauled the admitted murderer to an interview room. Farmer Page hurriedly confessed to the killer like a cardinal singing to the morning sun.

Page's story had started two years earlier. The gangster had hired Al Joseph to work at one of his gaming establishments but soon fired Joseph for bad conduct. Joseph disagreed and was fuming.

The word on the street was that Joseph was out to get Page. But it was more than that. Joseph was a member of the Spud Murphy gang in San Francisco. The gangster had bragged about how he would eliminate Page, thus clearing a path to take over gambling operations in Los Angeles.

Drinking into the wee hours at the Sorrento Café, an illegal liquor and gambling establishment in a stately Victorian mansion, Page saw Joseph. Joseph walked toward Page, then pushed his shoulder into his sworn enemy, yelling obscenities and threatening to kill him. Page shouted for him to back off. More words were exchanged. Suddenly, like a heavyweight boxer, Joseph threw a punch that landed, knocking Page to the ground. As he fought to get up, he saw his assailant go for his back pocket. Page figured it was for a gun, so he pulled his .38 semiautomatic caliber automatic pistol faster than Joseph, whose gun had gotten hung up on his pants. Page fired first, striking the young gambler in the back. The bullet clipped Joseph's heart, and he was dead before he hit the ground. With gun smoke still hanging in the air, Page and his entourage took off.

Bean wasn't impressed by this story and still booked Page. The wealthy gangster quickly posted his $50,000 bail and walked out of jail, back to his gambling operation. Three weeks later, the case appeared before Justice Russell, who promptly ruled Page innocent on the charge of murder. Russell held that the right of self-defense could not be denied any person, regardless of occupation or station, and that an overwhelming preponderance of evidence left him no alternative but to dismiss the case against Page. An angry Russell reiterated that there was no evidence to warrant any proceedings against Page and admonished the prosecution for bringing the matter before his court. Smirking, the Los Angeles gambling boss walked out of the courtroom a free man. A few hours later, Page was at an exclusive golf club bragging to the press about how he had lowered his score by three strokes.

A shooting between two known gangsters in Los Angeles made more than headlines. The spark reignited the flames of open vice and gambling. After just a few months in office, the new chief of police, R. Lee Heath (1924–1926), had to defend himself for allowing the Sorrento Café, a heavily barricaded, fully equipped liquor establishment, to operate in the heart of the Westlake residential district. The press raised the question: How many more were there if places such as the Sorrento Café of Bert the Barber ran undetected until the shooting? The media also demanded to know the number of armed gangsters thriving in LA right under the nose of police officials. Seemingly unfazed by the negative press, Heath stated that everyone should calm down, that everything was under control, and that there were no more such establishments.

Heath becoming chief of police had seemed preordained. Influential city leaders considered him the most influential politician in the department; without his cooperation, no others could succeed. A few years earlier, Chief Oaks had found this out the hard way when he tried to fire the politically entrenched Heath, then the captain of Central Division. Instead, Oaks was fired.

Heath was a contradiction. He did not look stern, as so many chiefs before had; he had a friendly face, gray hair, and steel-rimmed glasses that gave him the look of an English teacher, not the leader of a three-thousand-man police force. Heath's rise to the top had been steady and purposeful. He had been appointed patrolman in 1904, sergeant three years later, and just as quickly lieutenant. He was made captain in 1918. Heath later boasted that he enjoyed the "rigorous nature" of police work and the simple life it afforded. Like other officers of the era, he had earned $75 a month, with $2 deducted for pension. He worked seven days a week, with no days off, sick time, or overtime, and with only one two-week paid vacation each year. Officers had to purchase their own guns, handcuffs, blackjacks, and uniforms. Yet the labors of police work had not weighed him down. While steadily moving up the ranks, Heath had made time to earn a law degree from the University of Southern California. Despite department regulations to the contrary, he also developed strong connections to the city's political machine. Along the way, Heath befriended several men of questionable character, including Kent Kane Parrot.

The fatherly-looking Heath was like a Zen master preaching "reason, harmony, and cooperation" to the rank and file and instructing his men to be polite to citizens and to show respect to reporters. Unsurprisingly, one of his first executive decisions was to form the Bureau of Public Relations.

The troops responded to their innovative leader when they presented him with a gorgeous, jeweled badge and more flowers on the day of his promotion to chief than at a movie star's funeral. The privileged members of the elite Los Angeles Breakfast Club awarded the chief a gold badge and counted him as one of their own.

Heath strove to put more officers back on the street. To accomplish this, he asked the city council for thirty-three additional civilian employees to relieve patrolmen of clerical jobs so they could be assigned to patrol. The idea was way ahead of its time.

While ahead of his time in staffing, Heath was looking back in time when he brought back outlawed practices for the cop on the street. Once again, patrolmen could accept rewards (money citizens gave) and hand out "courtesy cards," and police badges to friends and privileged citizens. The cards allowed people to get out of traffic tickets. Citizens could flash these badges and stay out of jail for misdemeanor offenses.

Another procedural change invited corruption. A new regulation allowed felonies to be reduced to misdemeanors if done before the charges were filed. For example, prisoners arrested for felony drunken driving could be booked for being drunk, a low-level misdemeanor. Many arrestees remained in jail without being charged until they could raise enough money to hire an attorney and have the charges reduced. Some jailers persuaded prisoners to hire specific lawyers or use particular bail bondsmen, who they then gave the officers a kickback for the referral.

As chief, some in the press described Heath as a genius. He demonstrated again that a competent chief, free from political involvement, could improve the department's professionalism. During his one year as chief, August Vollmer had been able to force the politicians out of the LAPD's daily operations. Heath was no Vollmer. Under his command, politics again cast a shadow over the department. As it was for Chief Oaks, Heath would have to deal with the city's political boss, Kent Kane Parrot, and his "personal mayor," George E. Cryer. Parrot and Cryer worked to shape the LAPD into a department that furthered their individual needs and lined their pockets with cash.

With his law degree, Heath understood the importance of an educated police force. He took great pride in formally continuing Vollmer's ninety-day police school. The programs ensured that every recruit joining the LAPD would receive at least three months of training. And to ensure they were correctly schooled, Heath skillfully wrote much of the training curriculum.

Creating a permanent training school was significant, but getting qualified applicants into the program was challenging. Of those who applied, 75 percent were rejected for failing to meet the strict physical and mental requirements. The department made its expectations clear:

> If you do not make good within the next three months, if you fail to show that you will make a courageous, courteous, intelligent policeman of high moral character, with deep responsibility as to the position you hold, you will be dropped from the department.

But having a great training school did not deflect criticism from the Farmer Page shooting, which refused to go away and instead divided the city. It woke those who had been snoozing with dreams of a clean city. In an editorial, the *Times* pointed out that Page "is, after all, a product of a system; a system that has been growing stronger and bolder and eviler in Los Angeles during the last three or four years." The Page shooting directed public attention to the fact that he and others had been conducting gambling operations in LA on a scale of extraordinary proportions—no matter what denials came off the lips of politicians and police chiefs.

Jumping on the anti-Heath bandwagon (which was always good for political careers) was Councilman Robert Allan, who denounced Heath as being "absolutely indifferent" to gambling casinos. Allan further alleged that some of his internal investigators had been killed by gangsters or police officers who were attempting to prevent the investigators from learning the truth about the city's gambling rings. Heath was quick to respond: "Conditions are normal. There is bound to be vice, but so far as organized vice is concerned or any police protection for vice, there is nothing of that sort in Los Angeles." Those who supported Heath wrote off the hyperbole as "mere election propaganda." Chief Heath, at times, used the press to get the word out. When several criminals rented rooms in preparation for gambling in the city, the chief informed them through the media that they might want to try a different vocation.

> The time when they [vice lords] can open will never come while I am Chief of Police. These misguided gamblers are going to meet with a whole lot of bad luck if they try to open up. The lid will never be even slightly tilted while I am Chief and Los Angeles will never again see the day when it can be mentioned as an open town.

Chapter 10

Gangster versus Gangster Fight for Control of the Liquor Business

"If I die, I'm out of luck; if I get well, he will be out of luck."

—LA gangster

While the police were busy chasing after prostitutes and gamblers, a new type of criminal emerged as Prohibition sank its teeth into Americans' drinking habits. While rum runners were making millions unloading their illegal liquor on the beaches of Southern California or trucking it in, another type of criminal was taking note—the professional hijacker. These gangsters allowed the rum runners to do most of the work and then stole the whiskey at gunpoint while the illegal cargo was being transported. Reports of gunfire exchanged between speeding autos became as common as fireworks on the 4th of July. Bodies littered the city streets of Los Angeles like discarded trash.

Hijackers appeared along the coast of Southern California with shipments of whiskey from Canada. Heavily armed and operating with swift power boats and high-performance modified automobiles, the hijackers worked in groups of two to twelve men. The hijackers began attacking the rum runners and battling them for their liquor. Once Prohibition started, the hijackers' tactics evolved as they learned from their mistakes in the bloody confrontations with the equally dangerous rum runners. It was Gangsterism 101.

Initially, gunmen boarded the rum boats off the coast and often shot up the entire crew. With the guards out of the way, the hijackers landed the whiskey and sold it to their dealers in the city. This method of stealing ended abruptly when the shrewd rum runners mounted surplus military machine guns on their boat decks. In response, the hijackers altered their tactics. They took to fast-running boats and attacked the rum runners as they unloaded the loot on remote shorelines. This worked briefly until the rum runners began arming their men with the newly invented Thompson sub-machine gun. The firepower proved too much for the hijackers.

Leaving the water behind, the hijackers refined their attacks and located trucks traveling from the shore. The hijackers swooped in swift raids, ambushing the rum runners and, more often, getting away with the bottled gold.

But gangsters came in many forms. In some cases, hijackers ended up in shootouts with other gangs of hijackers as they attempted to deliver their stolen goods. In one reported case, rum runners hijacked a truckload of whiskey on the way to LA from San Pedro only to have a second group of hijackers attack fifteen minutes later and take control of the alcohol. As these hijackers entered LA, the original hijackers struck back and, in a furious firefight, managed to regain possession of the illegal cargo. The hijackings resulted in dead bodies spread throughout the streets and surrounding areas. In many cases, dead men were found in rooming houses and automobiles or were dumped in ditches. When arrests were made, no one talked. One dying suspect told a patrolman: "If I die, I'm out of luck; if I get well, he will be out of luck." The hijackers' words to the city were, "We will fight our battles." It was a clear warning to anyone wearing a badge.

Hijackings were becoming so common that LAPD plainclothes vice detectives were sometimes mistaken for hijackers as they raided the rum runners' hideouts. In one instance, acting on a tip, newly appointed Vice Captain James E. Davis, an up-and-coming fighter in the department who in a few short years would become the chief of police, oversaw just such a detail. Raiding a hideout in a residential area, Davis and his five handpicked men were met by two vicious dogs as they approached the house. Davis, always in the thick of things, took out one of the dogs as the group kept advancing. As they were about to enter the house, a barrage of shots narrowly missed the six men. Returning fire, the vice raiders arrested several men, captured hundreds of gallons of illegal liquor, and arrested the sniper for attempted murder. During the investigation, the criminals acknowledged they thought Davis and his officers were hijackers.

Gun battles between the police and rum runners on LA streets became as common as snarled traffic. When vice officers raided a home on West 79th Street, they were handcuffing one suspect when a second man ran away. As he sprinted from the house, he fired at pursuing officers and quickly jumped into a car. Two patrolmen gave chase. Catching up to the car as it sped through the busy city streets, the two officers fired twenty-five shots, riddling the back of the suspects' car but with no effect. As traffic thinned, the gangsters' car, powered by a large modified V-8 engine, soon was a dot in the distance as they escaped the slow-moving cop car. Once they had returned to the home, the officers were able to confiscate five-hundred gallons of moonshine.

Hijackers presented almost daily dangers to patrol officers. On patrol late at night, officers from University Division spotted a large sedan loaded with five people and what appeared to be six boxes of illegal liquor stacked in the car's open trunk. The patrolmen noted that the auto and its occupants fit the description of a notorious gang of hijackers operating in the Southwestern United States. As the two officers attempted to stop the vehicle, it abruptly sped away. The patrolmen gave chase and emptied their revolvers twice during the pursuit. But again, the modified car outdistanced the slower police car. Orders went out from the top to "shoot to kill" if the patrolmen spotted the hijackers again.

On the political front, positive reform steps were taken in 1925 by adopting a new city charter. This charter restored the ward system and raised the number of city council members from nine to fifteen. Terms in office were increased from two years to four. And in a notable achievement for the autonomy of the police department, the mayor no longer sat on the board of police commissioners. This was a progressive step in removing politics from the force. The number of police commissioners rose to five, with a staggered five-year term, meaning only one member could be replaced yearly. No longer could the mayor randomly remove commissioners without the city council's approval.

On the streets, a routine police call on Christmas Day 1925 introduced two individuals destined for local fame—both for the wrong reasons. Walking his beat, Patrolman T. Mayer was assigned a call to a bungalow court on South Westlake Avenue on a report of a fight. He was accompanied by a civilian friend, Richard Coster. The men walked to the location and found it quiet. As the two were leaving the interior courtyard, Albert Marco, a flamboyant underworld boss who ran a large prostitution ring, confronted the pair and got into words with the civilian, who stood his ground. With tempers rising, Marco unexpectedly pulled a gun from his pocket and threatened both men. Just as quickly as he drew his weapon, several of Marco's associates grabbed him and had him put his gun away—too late. Patrolman Mayer arrested Marco for felony assault with a deadly weapon and booked him into Central Jail. Two LAPD detectives later reduced the charge to a misdemeanor of disturbing the peace and allowed the gangster to post a $100 bail. The city prosecutor would not file the case and never explained why. Patrolman Mayer did not press the matter after an unnamed individual told him he would be fired if he testified against Marco.

The story made headlines and was turned into a political football thrown around by different councilmen as each argued his agenda. This quarrel in the papers introduced our second antagonist, Carl Jacobson, a stern city councilman who hailed from Norway. Through the press, Jacobson demanded that Chief Heath explain why Marco was given special treatment. Councilman Jacobson went on to claim many improprieties within the police force. Later, his actions would catapult him into the center of one of the most notable scandals in LAPD history.

In the chief's office, a different clash was taking place. All the success August Vollmer had achieved during his one year as chief was pretty much eliminated under the watch of Chief Heath. This was primarily because of orders from the mayor's office. Mayor Cryer reduced the LAPD's budget by 27 percent in 1926–1927. The budget decrease caused the ninety-day police academy to close, which was perhaps Vollmer and Heath's most significant accomplishment. When the training school closed, all formal recruit training stopped. The general caliber of recruits also declined, as did the shine of a more proficient LAPD; many of those who had gone through the ninety-day academy quit. Despite a sizable increase in the city's population, the city council refused to increase the department's size. Officers were again receiving near-poverty wages, and the department was once more generating headlines of corruption and vice payoffs within its ranks. The LAPD was headed downward, landing at its low point.

In the spring of 1926, Chief R. Lee Heath, having run the gamut from disgraced cop to chief of police, decided to put his law degree to work and retired from the police department. After a successful law career, he was ready to live out his life in the quiet neighborhood of Tujunga until he was "rediscovered" in the 1970s by an officer writing a history of the department. After that, the former chief became a frequent visitor to the department and shared some of his experiences with the official department historian at the time, George Wilson. Heath died in 1974 at the age of 93.

The next chief of police, James E. Davis, became synonymous with controversy and corruption, providing fodder for historians arguing his successes or failures since the day he was sworn in.

Chapter 11

First Edition
Chief James E. Davis

"You're fired!"

—Charles E. Sebastian, Chief of Police

Smelling fresh blooming flowers, along with fried bacon, James E. Davis had imagined this day since first pinning on his patrolman's badge fifteen years earlier. At just thirty-seven, Davis told anyone who would listen that he was about to become the youngest chief of police in the history of the Los Angeles Police Department. Neatly arranged on his spotless uniform were four gleaming gold stars. Sitting at the head table, along with outgoing Chief R. Lee Heath, Davis was surrounded by three-hundred doers and shakers of the most influential men in LA. This was the Los Angeles Breakfast Club, which had as members the wealthiest, most powerful, and most influential men in the City of Angels. Present on this blue-sky morning were notables such as Harry Chandler, real estate mogul and owner of the *Los Angeles Times*; writer Edgar Rice

159

Burroughs, famed "Tarzan" creator; oil industrialist Edward L. Doheny; and film trailblazers Louis B. Mayer, Darryl Zanuck, and Cecil B. De Mille. William Randolph Hearst had sent his representative, Guy Barham. United States Senator Samuel Shortridge and former Senator Frank Flint; Dr. Robert Millikan, the president of Cal Tech; and Dr. Rufus B. Von Kleinsmid, the president of USC, would not miss this history-making event.

The event was historic because for longer than people could remember, it was customary for chiefs of police to find themselves bereft of a job and indignantly go forth into the cold world, proclaiming their troubles to an "I already heard it" blasé public. Most of these chiefs were forgotten, like the last mayor. All too often, the new man was no admirer of the previous chief and was quick to indicate that his policies had been foolish and futile. Not this day. Outdoors under the shade of large trees, the outgoing chief stood as a leading member of the famed Breakfast Club, complimenting James Davis as he was to be the club's next president. For his part, Davis called Heath "the best chief of police Los Angeles ever had." It was a love fest.

Throughout the history of the Los Angeles Police Department, controversy and disagreement by historians have been standard, primarily when the discussion focuses on its leaders. It is not uncommon to have some historians praise a chief of police while others find serious fault. James E. Davis was the epitome of that kind of man. Davis served as chief of police for nearly nine years, making him fourth in the longevity of the fifty-seven chiefs of LAPD. This number is more stunning when one considers his tenure was during one of the most tumultuous and corrupt eras in Los Angeles history. Most historians have labeled him a corrupt chief that set the department back to the dark days. I would disagree. The answer is buried in a graveyard of facts with a headstone of corruption and an inscription of achievements.

To exhume the answer, one must start at the beginning and how Davis succeeded to chief at such a young age. Many would agree that your childhood has much to do with the individual you will become. For James Davis, this would be the exact case. Born in 1889 in Texas, the five-year-old child was experiencing the last of the Wild West when his family lived in Indian Territory among the Native American Choctaw people. Davis attended school until he was sixteen. His mother, who had an immense influence on him, was an ardent member of the Northern Methodist church and was fiercely opposed to liquor, card games, dancing, and the theater. Mention vice to her, and she would light up in different shades of red.

Davis recalled one day when the family was coming home from a Wednesday night prayer meeting. He saw, through an open doorway, couples dancing. "My mother seized my arm and pulled me away. 'Edgar,' she said, 'nevah, nevah, look at anything like that!'"

Mrs. Davis also passed on her repugnance of liquor. She was so strong in her preaching that Davis never drank or smoked his entire life. "I never saw liquor in our home except one time. My uncle hid a pint of whisky under the mattress, and my mother found it." Davis continued, "'Get out!' She told my uncle, 'And never come back!' He never did." His aversion to these "sins" would later serve him well as the head of LAPD's vice unit.

Religion was also foundational for Davis. His family prayed and read the Bible with each meal. Each day his mother would begin by reciting morning prayer and reading a short chapter from the Bible. At noon the family recited more prayers and usually read from Psalms. In the evening, they would pray and then read a long chapter from the Bible, usually from the New Testament. As Davis recalled: "On Sunday, we all went to church services and Sunday school, and of course to weekly prayer meetings. My Stepfather was a deacon and superintendent of the Sunday school." Perhaps it was all too much for the teenager. When he turned sixteen,

Davis got the wanderlust and ran away from home and all that religion.

Davis did not run far. He stayed in Texas, and his first job was as a hand on a cattle ranch. While the job sounds alluring, the future chief spent much time picking cotton. One day, the competitive Davis out picked almost everyone by gathering 435 pounds of cotton. Drifting around Texas and New Mexico, Davis worked as a clerk in express offices, at a grocery store, and as a homestead hand.

At nineteen, Davis felt the itch to travel beyond dusty Texas. But because he had little money, he did as generations of young men have done; he joined the Navy—or, at least, tried. The recruiter told him his heart was in bad shape. He traveled to Oklahoma to try to enlist again, and again a Navy recruiter told him he had a bad ticker. Never one to give up, Davis went to Dallas to join the Army. There, he was met with open arms and with no medical issues. Accepted into the Army, Davis was sent to Fort Sam Houston, where he had his sights on a cavalry regiment. Unfortunately for the teenager, there were no open positions.

The Army gave him three choices. He could join the infantry, the coast artillery, or a mountain gun battery. Davis, who pictured himself as a gallant cavalry soldier, did not want to join the infantry; besides, marching had no appeal.

So, Davis went to Wyoming, a state which was just about as young as he was. He decided he would join a mountain battery.

He arrived at Fort A. D. Russell and saw hundreds of mules in corrals. Those mules were used to transport a newly acquired weapon for the Army, a Vickers-Maxim 2.95-inch gun, each weighing 830 pounds when assembled. It took four mules to carry one heavy gun.

In 1908, with little time to train, the mountain battery was ordered to set sail for the Archipelago Islands because of the ongoing hostilities in the Philippine-American War. The battery members traveled on a slow-moving transport named the Buford, and it took over a month to arrive at their destination. En route, Davis stopped in Honolulu and hiked to the top of a mountain, which must've been a sight for a kid raised in a landlocked part of Texas.

In the Philippines, his unit was stationed at Mindanao Island, on the southernmost tip of the big islands, just seven degrees north of the equator. Davis spent the next year and a half there training and preparing for war. He was at 2,600 feet, which made breaking the mules and clearing a 250-mile stretch of mountainous terrain for their area of operations challenging. Davis recalled:

> I was thrown at least 200 times while we were breaking in those mules for monkey drill—mounting, vaulting, riding forward and facing rear at walk, trot, and gallop, and also knelling and standing. We were required to develop the same expertness at mule riding as for regular cavalry work. I got so I could fall without getting hurt.

Included in Davies' training, the battery played war games. In one memorable event, the unit was transported by ship to the other end of the island to stop the evading "Japanese" forces. Davis's transport ship had no place to dock, so it anchored offshore. The unit also had to figure out how to get the four-legged creatures to land. The quick-thinking soldiers solved that problem. The men threw the mules overboard, dove in after them, and guided them to shore. But some mules became so frightened that they turned and swam out to sea. Since Davis was the strongest swimmer in his troop, his job was to swim after these assess and turn them around.

By sunset, with the mules safely ashore, the battery loaded them with the large guns and hiked ten miles inland, spending the night camped out in a dry rice paddy field. The next day they marched twenty-five more miles to a strategic spot in the hills to "annihilate" the invaders. Having "won" the game, they hiked eighty miles back to camp. A short time later, Davis was promoted to corporal, raising his monthly pay to $28.80.

After three years in the Army, Davis yearned for new challenges. Despite having scarcely finished ninth grade, Davis was a calculating man with a strong intellect. So, when he was twenty-two and with just $15 in his pocket, Davis decided to become a Los Angeles police officer.

The man who would twice serve as the head of the LAPD found his way to Los Angeles in 1911. Stepping off the train in a perfectly ironed Army uniform with spit-shined boots, Davis was ready for a new life. With his dwindling life savings, the young man bought a new suit and applied for the department. In the early 1900s, getting on the force was difficult. The city's population had exploded, and five-hundred other men had the same idea. But as Davis would demonstrate then and throughout his life, he could use his acumen and drive to succeed to overcome obstacles. After testing, Davis finished among the top four candidates. Accepted onto the force, the newly minted officer used the remainder of his money to purchase his gun, handcuffs, brass buttons, uniform, and billy club. Davis hit the streets as a patrolman two months after arriving in LA. With a salary of $75 a month, the rookie patrolman was ecstatic. He had made it.

After a senior patrolman trained Davis for two shifts, Davis was turned loose in the streets in University Division. Almost immediately, he got into trouble. His family was in Texas, and he had no local friends. Davis felt isolated. On his first day on his beat, he met a mother with her pretty nineteen-year-old daughter. The rookie cop struck up a conversation with them that, over the days, led him to visit their home while on duty. Occasionally, he went inside or sat on the porch chatting. He later said: "It was silly—but I did it. Nobody had told me that it was highly improper and contrary to rule to visit with citizens I encountered on my beat. This acquaintance—it was perfectly ordinary friendship."

Soon the neighbors were gossiping about Davis visiting this house, especially since the woman's husband was at work when Davis showed up. When the husband heard about it, he went straight to police headquarters and complained. When two sergeants showed up to interview the mother and daughter, they both told the investigators that Davis was "a pest." After the inquiry, police officials determined that Davis had violated department rules and was ordered before Chief Sebastian, who promptly fired him. Standing at attention before the chief, Davis was tight-lipped: "I was used to accepting orders without question, so

I took my dismissal without a word." A demoralized Davis handed his badge to the chief and slowly walked out the door and away from the LAPD.

Distancing himself from Los Angeles and his failure, Davis took up residence in Arizona. Here he wore the badge of a streetcar conductor. Almost like a gypsy, the dispirited Davis continued his trek east, looking for something he would enjoy as much as being an LAPD officer. Tired of working as a machinist's assistant and other backbreaking jobs, Davis decided to try and get back on the LAPD and wrote Chief Sebastian. He gave details of the incident that had gotten him fired and begged for a second chance. The chief consented, and by the summer of 1912, Davis was again a member of the LAPD. He later stated: "I was determined at that time to go as far as I could in the service and wipe out any false opinions that had been built up about me." Like a losing football coach always looking over his shoulder for his replacement, Patrolman Davis was driven never to allow anything to jeopardize his career. He became a strict enforcer of the law and a model officer.

Back on the job, Davis was hand-picked by Sergeant A.W. Gifford and two other men to comprise a new vice unit. They were tasked with raiding lottery establishments, gambling houses, high prostitution areas, and the places bootleggers worked. Although Prohibition was still years away, in 1912, the Gandier ordinance fixed a $100 minimum fine for selling, serving, or giving away liquor without a license.

Davis was just twenty-three. He weighed 150 pounds but looked lighter because of his compact build. Thanks to his mom, the young man had strict moralistic views on vice, which made him the perfect fit for this vice unit. Sergeant Gifford took advantage of Davis's physical prowess, asking Davis to use his attributes to find ways to enter the criminal establishments and gain an advantage.

The young vice officer loved these assignments and performed his duties brilliantly. But after two months, the unit was disbanded, and Gifford and his crew were reassigned to patrol. Such was the life of honest vice officers in the LAPD.

Back walking a beat, Patrolman Davis would not repeat past mistakes. In short time, he had the highest arrest rate on his watch. In one month alone, his misdemeanor arrests resulted in jail sentences totaling over three thousand hours. His specialty was getting weapons off the street. Davis made it a practice to search everyone who looked even a little suspicious. He removed scores of guns and knives from these armed suspects.

Davis developed a specialty with "knife wielders," whom he found liked to carry them up their sleeves, inside their collars, and even between their legs. His favorite move when he suspected someone was carrying a knife was to grab the person's wrist and run his hands up and down the suspect's arms. In just one month on night watch, along with his partner, Davis said, "We took 86 concealed weapons from pedestrians whom we stopped." He estimated that they searched 2,500 men on one shift.

His biggest catch while working his beat came when he had a chance meeting with a lost woman. As he gave her directions, he thought about how nice she was. Two months later, Davis was off-duty and saw the woman again. After a few dates, Davis was smitten. The following year, Davis married Edna R. Kline. They were a happy couple, eventually having five children and a life-long marriage. I interviewed June Davis, the youngest of these siblings, years later.

Davis's experiences in life prepared him for being under fire. He knew what it was to have the muzzle of a gun stuck into his ribs or to chase armed suspects down dark alleys. He had also been in a gunfight. But the nearest he ever came to having his obituary printed between a black border in the *Daily Bulletin* was when he was working the Chinatown squad.

During a pawnshop robbery, a young Mexican shot the owner. Running into the street to escape, the killer found his route blocked by Patrolman Teddy McAuliffe, who had heard the gunshot and came running. The suspect saw the responding officer and shot him. McAuliffe went down with a bullet in his foot. As this happened, a citizen approached, and the suspect shot him. At the same time, a patrolman named Condaffer was riding past on a streetcar and, seeing the suspect and the downed officer, jumped off and gave chase. He pursued the suspect for a block but lost him.

Davis was on duty in Chinatown with his partner, Patrolman Button. They were sitting in a makeshift substation, which was a small tin shack about eight by ten feet when Patrolman Condaffer came running up and, breathing heavily, asked if they had seen a Mexican with a gun run past. They had not, but the trio decided to split up to search the area where the suspect was last seen. Just moments later, Davis heard multiple gunshots. As he ran towards the sound, he saw gun flashes inside a Chinese rooming house.

As Davis came to the doorway, Condaffer came stumbling down the stairs holding his arm; blood was everywhere. Shots continued to ring out from the second floor. Running up the stairs, Davis saw his partner, Officer Button, at the top, but he was not shooting. "My gun is jammed," he yelled. Officials would later discover that a bullet from the suspect's gun had smashed the barrel of Button's gun. The suspect had shot Button in his shooting arm, and he had dropped his revolver.

Sneaking a peek around the corner of the hallway, Davis, the only officer not shot, saw the suspect. He fired three shots at him, missing. With a pause in the gunfire, Davis charged down the hallway at the killer. As he ran, Davis fired three more shots, double action, as fast as he could. He again missed. With no more bullets, Davis watched as the Mexican dodged into a room. Looking into the room, Davis saw the man hastily loading three cartridges into his gun's cylinder. As Davis charged in, the suspect slammed shut the cylinder and pulled the trigger three times but landed on empty chambers. Davis later said, "If he hadn't been so nervous, he might have thrown the cylinder so the trigger would have snapped on cartridges instead—and I wouldn't be here now."

With no bullets left, Davis smashed the barrel of his gun over the suspect's head, knocking the killer unconscious, fracturing his skull, and bending the barrel of his sidearm. Davis later had his revolver repaired and carried it for the rest of his career.

Looking at national events, Davis thrived during Prohibition. Corruption was rampant throughout society and within the Los Angeles Police Department. In just one year, between 1922 and 1923, more than one hundred officers from the twelve-hundred-member force were discharged for corruption and brutality. By remaining honest yet resourceful, James E. Davis stood out and was noticed by those attempting to reform the department. He also did not use politics to promote himself. Davis took nine years to make sergeant but thereafter made a meteoric rise through the ranks. As Davis put it: "About the time I was made detective lieutenant, I suddenly woke up and began to study what was going on ahead of me in the management of the Police Department."

To better himself, Davis requested assignments to every detail of the detective bureau, from homicide to pickpocketing to bunko, so that he could become familiar with all phases of these jobs. Soon the Texan went from sergeant to captain of vice. His promotions corresponded to the department's expansions. As the population in Los Angeles tripled during the 1920s, the city added nine-hundred new patrolmen. By 1930, the city had reached 1.5

million citizens. It would not be long before Davis would protect and serve this ever-expanding population.

In 1924, shortly after R.L. Heath became chief of police, Davis was in command of the vice division. Davis set new records of arrests for liquor, gambling, and red-light violations during his two years as commander. When interviewed about these stunning statistics, Davis said:

> We not only piled up the greatest totals of arrests for these offenses to date, but we also obtained the highest percentage of convictions for vice offenses in the history of the department. In 1925 we arrested more than 3,700 Wright act violators, of whom 94.6 percent were convicted, and in red-light, gambling and lottery cases we had a conviction rate of 98 to 99 percent.

These numbers were no fluke due to the restructuring of the vice division. To accomplish a reorganization in the most corrupt division within the LAPD speaks to Davis's management skills. For decades, vice had many corrupt officers on the take. Vice lords understood paying off the cops as an operating expense. Davis knew this, as he had seen it firsthand throughout his career.

Consequently, he chose men assigned to vice duty who would not easily be corrupted. Davis instituted a system of duplicating all vice reports from citizens, with one copy going to police headquarters while the other stayed in the reporting division. In the past many complaints were never followed up on; this system changed that.

Davis further required officers receiving information about bootlegging, gambling, and vice activities to turn them into Central Station. In the reports, they had to document the complaints and their actions to resolve the issues. The record bureau duplicated these complaints in triplicate and sent copies to Central Division, the district attorney's office, and the federal prohibition unit. Davis determined that violators would have more difficulty arranging for or getting protection when three entities had copies of reports indicating what occurred.

Davis made additional changes based on his own experiences in vice. He required officers making vice arrests to collect evidence and turn in detailed case reports. The city prosecutor's office used these reports to check each case as they were presented in court. If any pertinent facts or evidence in the officer's original report failed to show up when the case was tried, Davis called the officer in for thorough questioning. If the patrolman failed to turn over all the evidence to the prosecutor, whether facts or exhibits in his possession, he was "properly disciplined."

On February 25, 1926, Chief Heath announced he would resign on April 1. Davis had no idea. He was at his desk when he heard a commotion and saw a familiar reporter darting around desks, headed towards him. The anxious reporter asked Davis what his plans would be as chief of police. This was how Davis learned he was headed to the top of the LAPD, on the recommendation of outgoing Chief Heath. Most officers witnessing the discussion between Davis and the reporter event believed that this had to be the first time in department history that a chief had been appointed without his knowing it, and the mayor had not made the choice.

Sworn in as the youngest chief of police in LAPD history on April 1, 1926, Davis hit the pavement running. His first order of business was to reintroduce professionalism and esprit de corps into each department entity. He accomplished this by continuing and expanding the curriculum at the three-month police-training school. Chief August Vollmer had created the school; Chief Heath had continued it until funding had fallen through. Chief Davis wanted to start it up again. As he told the press: "You'll be glad to know, that the old roughneck policeman is fast becoming a thing of the past...We are developing a police force whose object is not only to serve the public, but also serve it with the courtesy and consideration to which it is entitled." With his military background, the new chief understood the necessity of having his officers look the part. "Within the next few days look your favorite police officer over for new and surprising refinements. Every day every policeman must report for duty with shoes that show the effects of recent elbow grease, and a uniform well-cleaned and pressed."

When Davis joined the department, training consisted of giving policemen their badges and starting them out on their beats, sometimes with a veteran officer. In his first speech to the graduating class of the police training school, the chief set the stage for the LAPD's changing of the guard:

> You have asked for the position of being one of the force of trained men who protect the lives and property of the people of Los Angeles. You have applied to the Civil Service Commission and passed the commission's mental and physical examinations. You have spent three months in the Police Training School, where you have secured the beginnings of the knowledge of the law, of crime prevention and detection, first aid to the injured and much other information that a modern policeman must know. You have passed the severe mental and physical examination given you in the training school You will now be given three

months training in actual police work. You have made good thus far If you do not make good within the next three months, if you fail to show that you will made a courageous, courteous, intelligent policeman of high moral character, with deep responsibility as to the position you hold, you will be dropped from the department, You have my best wishes to make good.

No wonder the Bureau of Research in Washington, DC, recommended law enforcement agencies adopt the LAPD training structure for their departments.

With the training school running smoothly, Davis focused on reducing traffic deaths and reducing vice in the city. In both areas, he was unsuccessful, but he learned a valuable lesson: to succeed in far-reaching projects, he needed the public's support.

At this time, it was common practice for street cops to issue "courtesy cards" to their best friends and acquaintances. If stopped for a minor traffic offense, they could produce the signed business card and get out of a ticket. "If a courtesy card means that certain citizens are to be accorded special privileges in violation of the law," Davis said, "that practice must be discontinued immediately." He added there would also be no "squaring" (fixing) of traffic tickets for friends so they could avoid paying fines.

Regarding traffic enforcement in the city, the chief ordered that anyone traveling over 28 mph should be cited to cut down on traffic accidents. Davis reasoned that even a slow-reacting motorist could brake in time to avoid a fatal accident. A municipal judge supported his reasoning, and he started issuing heavy fines for those cited for speeding. Within just six weeks, the accident rate had dropped 60 percent. But the public protested the citing of so many speeders. Just as quickly as Davis had instituted his plan to reduce accidents, the judge who had enforced the changes was transferred to San Pedro, and a more lenient judge was placed in traffic court. Soon the accident rate was back to where it had been, and Davis said: "Thus ended my first big experiment as chief."

Davis's second test was in vice enforcement. Chief Davis beefed up his vice division to 135 officers. He believed the public would support his attempt to eradicate commercialized vice. He again piled up heavy arrest totals. Many offenders were arrested so often that they left town in disgust.

The courts were the first to rebel. Offenders who Davis and his vice men thought should do jail time instead got small fines and were released. Next, the newspapers opposed the chief. One newspaper criticized Davis for keeping too many men in vice enforcement instead of criminal investigations. "It is the primary duty of police to protect life and property; enforcement of sumptuary laws is secondary and trivial by comparison." Even the reform-minded churches, for the most part, were either neutral or opposed.

As Davis squirmed at police headquarters, he voiced his disbelief. "I had expected applause from the churches when I began the vice campaign; I got only silence and opposition…Just as with traffic law enforcement, I found that I had no real general support. I had succeeded in winning the opposition of the underworld and the Christian element as well, despite giving Los Angeles the best liquor law enforcement of any American city." With these double failures, the law and order chief took off his gloves; he was done playing paddy-cake with the criminal element; instead, he would break out his big guns.

Chapter 12

Gangsters Beware
There's a New Chief in Town

"I want them brought in dead, not alive. I'll reprimand any officer who shows the least mercy to a criminal."

—Chief James E. Davis

As darkness was falling on the City of Angels, three of the LAPD's elite detectives, Lieutenant Charles Hoy, Lieutenant Richard Lucas, and Officer Ellis Bowers, met to discuss their strategy for a stakeout scheduled for later that night. The men were from the elite robbery and vice unit. They were reacting to a tip from a citizen who believed that car thieves would attempt to steal an expensive automobile parked in the person's rear-locked garage. The detectives' interest was not so much the car but the garage filled from floor to ceiling with bootleg liquor. The trio of detectives had received word from the street that the gangster Harry "Mile Away" Thomas was going for the loot. These men knew Thomas well. He had previously been arrested nine times, including twice for murder. His nickname came from his alibi. When he was arrested, he would say he had been a "mile away" when the crime occurred.

The officers went heavily armed, one with a machine gun and the other with a shotgun loaded with buckshot. Each also carried revolvers on their hips. The detectives took up positions in the darkened garage at 1408 West Thirty-Fifth Street. On the third night of their stakeout, around 8 pm on April 21, 1927, the officers heard someone prying the lock on the garage door. Outside, they could just make out "a dark form" between the slits in the garage's wood. Suddenly, the door flew open, and a man entered, holding a flashlight in one hand and a gun in the other. As a beam of light illuminated him, Lieutenant Lucas yelled, "Stick 'em up!" Thomas, silhouetted in the doorway, fired two quick shots at Lucas. "That is when we let him have it," Lucas later stated. Flashes from the gunfire lit up the garage as bullets rained down on Thomas. Mile Away was hit six times: three times in the chest, two times on his left side, and once in the hand. Although he should have been dead where he fell, Thomas managed to run out of the garage and through the yard before collapsing in the arms of a patrolman stationed on the perimeter.

On the ride to the hospital, Lucas told Thomas he was dying and attempted to elicit a dying declaration.

"Everybody has to fall sometime," Thomas muttered, expiring a few moments later.

The next day, two LA newspapers wrote it was a "setup" by LAPD to get Thomas. Chief Davis answered the criticism. He defended the officers by saying Thomas had shot first, and they were protecting themselves. "I want them brought in dead, not alive. I'll reprimand any officer who shows the least mercy to a criminal. That's my answer to those who do not like the way 'Mile Away' Thomas was killed."

Davis was tired of gangsters shooting up his city. As other chiefs had done before him, Davis declared war on the criminals inundating Los Angeles. Davis specifically targeted the "professional gangster and killers" who had been brought in to serve as bodyguards and protectors of bootleggers and hijackers:

> The problem of the professional murderer and gunman has grown to such serious proportions here in Los Angeles that the police department with its present equipment can no longer cope with it efficiently. The citizens here are entitled to greater protection than it is possible for us to give...They (gangsters) work in automobiles capable of leaving the police cars far behind when they are pursued.

> Two of our best officers have lost their
> lives at the hands of gunmen only recently.

The chief went before the police commission and asked for two armored automobiles for his officers' safety. He also wanted the armored cars modified so his officers could keep up with the criminals. Inside these new "wheeled forts," as the press called them, would be crews of hand-picked rifle and pistol shots who were instructed to "shoot to kill all hijackers, gangsters, and bootleggers attempting to evade arrest." The police commission liked the idea and approved the chief's request.

Just months in office, Chief Davis went after his other nemesis, the rum runners. "I am going to teach the gun-toting element and the rum smugglers operating in this vicinity that the Police Department intends to use its every resource to cure the city of murders and the resultant evils of the liquor trade…These men are not going to turn Los Angeles into another Chicago."

During Prohibition (1920–1933), criminals had perfected their illegal alcohol distribution process. This criminal configuration netted them a cool $10 million annually and unofficially became one of California's leading industries, albeit illegal. These crooks were also arrogant. They did not think of themselves as bootleggers or rum runners but as "importers" of primarily premium Scotch whiskey brought in from Canada.

For several years, the criminals basked in financial success. They used vast sums of money to bribe anyone who might get in their way. From the mob bosses to city councilmen to cops on the take, everyone was happy— everyone, that is, except Davis.

As a veteran of the war in the Philippines and a savvy street cop, Davis understood combat. He laid out a plan similar to a wartime battle plan: maximize your troops and hit at the heart of the enemy. It proved effective. Davis caused the rum runners more trouble, expense, and direct loss in a few years than any other law enforcement agency before or since.

His plan was calculated to wear down the mobsters' desire to commit crimes in Los Angeles. The chief called it "rousting." Rousting was flooding the streets with cops and arresting the rum runners and criminals for anything illegal, no matter how minor. While it was deemed unlawful in most legal circles, Davis continued rousting because "it worked" by keeping the criminals off the streets, giving them little time to shoot up the city.

The rousting squad was hand-picked by Davis and was made up of tough, beefy, robust cops who looked much like the bad guys they were arresting. Davis's strategy involved leaking the word that the police department was about to hunt the criminal element nonstop. At the same time, Davis's two specially trained Liquor Squads would be on the streets, armed with machine guns and using photographs to identify the best-known rum runners.

As the squad located the criminals, they arrested them, handcuffing them, loading them into a patrol wagon, and escorting them to jail. At the station, policemen booked the criminals for whatever seemed appropriate, but primarily for vagrancy. In a few hours, mob attorneys appeared with writs secured through the local courts, and the prisoners were released. Chief Davis expected this and made it part of his strategy. No sooner had the rum runners and mobsters returned to the streets than the Liquor Squads would find them and arrest them again. The entire process started over again. During "rousting time," these men might be arrested six times a week and behind bars for as many as two days. It did not take long, and the criminals realized they would be charged whenever they were found on the streets.

The system became so successful that when a rousting was announced, criminals would form a line at Central Station to say that they "had quit the game" and were selling real estate or working at some local store—in their efforts not to be arrested. While the police were making scores of arrests, members of Davis's other handpicked squad were out looking for warehouses where criminals stored whiskey. Detectives tried to gather enough evidence to convict the criminal bosses for much longer terms than two days.

Under Chief Davis's leadership, the LAPD successfully drove out the rum runners through rousting. The rum runners and mobsters had enough, and most relocated to where the pickings were less contested. They settled in cities well away from Los Angeles and as far away from the LAPD and Chief Davis as they could get.

Chapter 13

The Man with the Red Underwear

"I'll put a bullet in my brain. I realize I'm through."

—Councilman Carl Jacobson

Even today, it is enough to make a grown man blush. It was a Norwegian bespectacled city councilman pitted against a trigger-happy mobster who just as soon shoot you as to look at you. Councilman Carl Jacobson was a teetotaler. He did not drink because he disliked everything about liquor and what it stood for. His life was devoted to removing all vice from the streets of LA. Gangster Albert Marco was a racketeer, pimp, and extortionist who intensely disliked anyone questioning his profession. The clash between these two diametric opposed men was hard to grasp, even in the corrupt city of Los Angeles.

Jacobson moved to LA in 1909. Earlier, he had been an engineer for the Southern Pacific Railroad. He ran for city council in 1925 but lost by twelve votes to Joseph Fitzpatrick, who, shortly after the election, lost his seat over receiving a bribe. The city council then appointed Jacobson to the vacant seat. The newly appointed councilman declared his disdain for the entrenched organized crime syndicate in Los Angeles in his opening salvo as a city official. He proclaimed he would rid the streets of prostitution, bootleggers, and gamblers—everything Albert Marco stood for and profited from.

Marco had immigrated from Italy in 1908, arriving through Ellis Island. Marco had become a pimp and con man in Nevada. Along the way, he went to prison but was quickly released and headed to Los Angeles in a Cadillac overflowing with illegal liquor. The gangster liked what he saw and decided to take up residence. In 1925, the hot-tempered hoodlum had pulled a gun on a city patrolman. But before he could shoot, his cronies had stopped him. He was arrested for assault with a deadly weapon, but Marco, with his paid connections, had gotten off and had his gun returned. The police officer refused to testify for fear of losing his job or life.

It was clear to Marco who on the city council had to be pointed in another direction—Carol Jacobson. Marco offered Jacobson $25,000 ($370,000 in today's money) to find another cause to pursue. Jacobson would have nothing to do with the bribe and reported Marco to the feds. This led to Marco receiving a quarter-million-dollar fine. The gangster was not deterred and tried another approach—one that was very spiteful.

The nastiness started with an anonymous complaint to LAPD vice detectives about a "wild party" at 4372 Beagle Street. Suspicions should have been made if any honest official had taken notice of the police response to a simple party. A typical vice response included a sergeant and three detectives, but this routine call drew Captain Bert Wallis, vice division commander; Captain Frank Williams, commander of the intelligence division; Detective Ricard Lucas; and the often-fired Special Investigator Harry Raymond. As the quartet rushed out the door, they took the time to call two *Times* reporters, asking the reporters to join them.

Staked out at the house on Beagle Street, they saw a man arrive and enter the house. The cops slowly crept up to a window and peeked in. According to their subsequent report, they saw Councilman Jacobson sprawled on the bed next to a beautiful nude woman, wearing only his flashy red underwear. On the table was a bottle of whiskey and two glasses. Before the police entered the house, one officer went to the fuse box and turned out the lights by cutting power to the house. Then the six men burst into the tiny home. With flashbulbs popping and flashlights blazing, Los Angeles City Councilman Carl Jacobson and his partner were arrested for lewd conduct. Jacobson asked for one of the detectives' guns. "I'll put a bullet in my brain. I realize I'm through," he said. "I'm only human."

But Jacobson, or the "Marco nemesis," as he was known, quickly snapped out of his shock. When asked to sign a confession, the councilman refused, saying, "This is a frame-up." The LAPD officers replied that "The police did not lead him out there or remove his clothes or those of the woman."

The vice officers' story started to unravel when uninvolved detectives discovered that the nude woman, who had given her name as Helen Ferguson, was actually Callie Grimes. She was the sister-in-law of Frank Cox, who worked in the LAPD vice division. Cox worked for Captain Wallis, one of the raiders and a unit commander. Understanding where the investigation was going, the police offered to withdraw the charge if the councilman would sign an affidavit admitting his guilt. He bitterly refused. Let the trial begin.

Jacobson admitted to having an "immoral interest" in Grimes at the trial but steadfastly denied he ever acted upon his feelings. After he refused a drink (he was a teetotaler), he testified that the lights went out, and the detectives came rushing in.

Grimes, who Marco's attorney represented, took the stand with all the confidence of women who knew just where this trial was going. "He (Jacobson) said he had admired me from the first minute he saw me and that I was a beautiful woman. He talked about 'dying for love' and complained because his wife was too religious." The police stuck with their story of receiving a call for a wild party. When they responded, based on their observations, they arrested Jacobson for entering a room for immoral purposes.

As the jury—eleven women and one man—filed into court after deliberations, they reported they were hopelessly deadlocked (seven to five for conviction). The DA decided to refile the case. Before the second trial began, all charges were dropped against the city councilman when prosecutors had serious doubts about police evidence and their testimony. Under a remaining cloud of suspicion and doubt, Jacobson retained his seat on the city council. Meanwhile, Ms. Grimes left LA with a new boyfriend and the $2,500 she had received from Marco in her purse. In addition to this money, Marco had promised her $100 a month for life. She was set.

Marco could not stay out of trouble. Like most of his encounters with police, this encounter occurred early in the morning, this time at Ships Café, a boat-shaped speak-easy located on the Venice Pier. Getting into an argument with a patron, Marco made slanderous remarks about a woman in their group. The patron and Marco exchanged words, and a brawl ensued between the two men. With his fiery temper unchecked, Marco pulled his gun, shot the man, and seriously injured another. Marco was hauled off to jail, kicking and screaming at the police, the patrons, and anyone else within earshot.

Stuck behind bars, Marco either forgot or could not make his monthly payment of $100 to Ms. Grimes. Not a good thing.

In November 1928, Grimes was back in LA and broke. She blew the whistle on Marco. Grimes testified at a grand jury investigation that Marco had told her he wanted Jacobson destroyed and removed from his seat on the city council. Grimes explained how much he would pay her if she got the councilman into a compromising position. The grand jury indicted Marco, his associate Charlie Crawford, and police officers Wallis, Lucas, Raymond, and Cox on charges of criminal conspiracy.

The jury was hung 11 to 1 for conviction at the subsequent trial. When evidence was presented of jury tampering, prosecutors filed for another trial. This time, the prosecution proved that Grimes had met with Lucas and Raymond before she and Jacobson had met at the house, and the cops had already been waiting for two hours.

Jacobson, for the first time, told the court how when the lights had gone out in the house, the police must have hit him from behind, knocking him unconscious. When he shook the cobwebs from his head, he saw Captain Wallis holding his trousers. This point had both sides arguing whether someone had removed the councilman's pants. The jury came back deadlocked for a second time, six to six. After another jury tampering allegation, the case was scheduled to go before another jury, but Buron Fitts, the district attorney, had had enough lying witnesses and withdrew all charges. The case was over.

The police commission removed Wallis, Williams, and Cox. But just as quickly, the city attorney reinstated the policemen, saying their civil service protections had been violated. For others, the outcome was not as pleasant. Richard Lucas, who reportedly did all "the dirty work" of setting up Jacobson, was forced to resign. And for a second time, Harry Raymond, the consistently disgraced cop, was again removed from the department. A few years later, he was the principal witness in a corruption case against LAPD's Intelligence Division. Marco stood trial on other charges—this time of the assault and attempted murder—and was convicted. He was sent back to Italy. Jacobson served on the city council until 1933 when he resigned to sell real estate. The citizens of Los Angeles were again left wondering who the real crooks were.

James Davis had reason to feel insecure as the department head. With LAPD chiefs of police lasting an average of just eleven months, Davis wanted to keep his position and eliminate criminals from the streets of Los Angeles. After spending two years at the top, Davis could point out that all major crimes were down. As the *Times* wrote, officers appeared very disciplined, and "promotions appear to have been made based on merit and fitness, and there has been a noticeable decrease in politics by department members."

The young, energetic chief constantly fought against corruption within the ranks. Each corrupt officer removed from the department cleared the way for an improved professional force where most men were striving to make the

LAPD a career, not just a job. The *Times* proclaimed that Chief Davis was making a difference:

> There has never been a time in the history of the Los Angeles police department when there appeared to be less ground for suspicion of organized corruption allied with crime and vice than there is at the present moment. Neither the personal integrity nor the personal habits of Chief Davis have furnished just ground for criticism and if there is any grafting on the part of individual officers, it is not because of the head of the department or of any on the other high ranking officers.

But the public was riled less by reduced crime or rogue cops cashing in on corruption. Instead, they were concerned with vice, which drove headlines and ended careers. As chief, Davis fine-tuned vice operations to make divisional commanders responsible for illegal activity within their geographic boundaries. Each captain reported directly to the chief. Divisional commanders could no longer sit on the sidelines and do nothing about the vice in their streets. This was an improvement, but the reformers in the city were never completely satisfied; they believed the LAPD was not dedicating the staff needed to clean things up. The progressives found a spokesman for their cause in a backwoods preacher who wanted a change at the top—to remove Chief Davis.

Robert Shuler, who earned the nickname "Fighting Bob," was an American evangelist and political figure. He used the pulpit of his Southern Methodist Church to spread his messages about corruption, crime, vice, and abuses within the city. The LAPD was one of his favorite targets. Starting in the late 1920s and continuing through the early 1930s, Fighting Bob led one of the nation's most controversial religious radio stations. Shuler was king of the city even if other ministers criticized him while newspapers deplored him. Criminals wanted nothing to do with him. Politicians shook in their boots when Shuler mentioned their names. The public could not get enough of his fire and brimstone. Wherever his righteous finger pointed, the person being singled out could only pray for forgiveness.

Fighting Bob was born in 1880 to a Methodist minister in Virginia. Ordained by the time he was twenty-three, he traveled the hills and hollows of Kentucky and Tennessee before moving to LA in 1920 with his wife and six children. His timing was perfect. Parishioners liked the uncompromising evangelical revival then sweeping the nation and wanted more. Fighting Bob delivered.

The reverend accused Davis of protecting vice and failing to rid the department of graft and corruption. Davis, in turn, blamed the district attorney and the courts for being uneven in prosecuting vice arrest. The chief pointed out that the law set specific penalties, yet most judges levied fines far below the legal minimum. Davis was right. Certain prosecutors and some judges' loyalties were to the underworld. Additionally, many jurists received bribes to tilt the justice system in favor of the criminal element.

In 1929, an election year in Los Angeles, it was a time when the chief of police became anxious. The LAPD again became a target of the candidates running for mayor—a favorite target every election. Cryer had lost Parrot's support; Parrot had ensured that Cryer had never lost an election since 1921, so not having Parrot's support, Cryer withdrew from the race. John Porter, a board member of the Los Angeles County Church Brotherhoods, had the backing of Robert Shuler, which helped ensure his victory. A new mayor typically maneuvered to get in a new man as chief. Porter did not, at least not right away. In fact, he stood behind Chief Davis despite the firestorm brought on by Shuler's allegations there was corruption and open vice conditions in the city. Fighting Bob demanded that Mayor Porter sack the chief.

Porter refused and said he would not allow Davis to be "railroaded" out of office on "gossip and rumor." Through his radio broadcast, the powerful Shuler told his listeners that he had "worn his knees nearly to the bone praying for the mayor" and was "cut to the heart" by the mayor's statements on Davis. The reverend said the mayor lacked a backbone. Porter said he appreciated having Shuler's support during the election and that he "liked him" but made it clear where he stood with the incumbent chief:

> I do not desire a break with him [Shuler] but I repeat that Chief Davis has co-operated with me in the cleaning the police department of graft and corruption. Months ago, I made a private investigation of rumors against the chief and found no proof to sustain these charges. My mind toward the chief is open and I shall not ask his dismissal unless he is shown to be guilty of charges.

Although Mayor Porter initially backed Davis, his support was tenuous. In 1929, a smattering of headline-grabbing events increased the pressure to fire Davis. The Jacobson case had dragged on, keeping all the damaging information public. There also were many reports of police brutality that Davis had to answer. Like many other police officials, he was inclined to excuse policemen who beat citizens when "they had it coming." His usual reply was: "Officers are only human and can't be expected to stand unlimited abuse." But the chief did not hesitate to fire an officer if the patrolman had beaten a citizen severely or without justification. Sergeant Earl F. Chandler, while interrogating a robbery suspect, became upset with the accused, beating him and knocking out three of the man's teeth in the interrogation room at Wilshire Station. After reviewing the case, Davis fired the sergeant only to have the police commission order him to return to full duty after leveling a fine of two months' pay. To respond, Davis issued a department-wide bulletin forbidding violence:

> The use of force or violence upon a prisoner for any other purpose than in self-defense, or in overcoming resistance to arrest, or to prevent an escape, is strictly forbidden. Securing statements or confessions by the use of threat of force or violence is likewise forbidden. If any officer is found guilty of using force or violence upon a prisoner for any reason other than the three noted above, drastic action will be taken.

Eventually, it was not police brutality but the LAPD vice unit that would turn public sentiment from whispers into shouts for the resignation of Chief of Police James E. Davis.

At the time, the department operated vice units in two squads. One was led by Captain Clyde Plummer, who had an excellent record against rum runners, hijackers, and bootleggers. He was also an uncompromising, honest leader. The other squad was led by the once-fired Max Berenzweig, appointed by Davis but had no formal rank as he could not pass the civil service exam. Many men under his command were involved in extortions from Harry D. "Bathhouse" McDonald, who ran a large bootlegging operation. When McDonald was arrested and started to name police department members whom he was paying off, Berenzweig fled the city.

Little is known of Max Berenzweig, but since Davis hired the former disgraced cop, it deserves a closer look. The first reference to Berenzweig was in 1919 when Chief Butler dismissed him as "unfit" to be a "special policeman." During the early 1920s, he continually appeared in newspaper accounts as a person who had an avid interest in police work. He loaned out his automobiles to gain favor with the department and went along on raids. By 1924 under Chief Heath, he was called "Lieutenant Berenzweig" in the newspapers. Later, Captain Clyde Plummer, the straight-shooting vice commander, fired him for at least the second time in the decade for being unfit for duty. But for reasons that are not clear, Davis hired him back, bypassing civil service, and made him a special agent working alongside Plummer, who had earlier fired him. The chief raised eyebrows when he put him in charge of the second vice unit.

The question arises of why Davis would hire a known unqualified questionable officer from the past. Perhaps Davis knew of Berenzweig back in his days on vice and thought highly of a civilian who would donate some of his personal property to the department. There is no evidence that Davis knew he was still a crook at the time of his appointment. In other similar instances, Davis would give a fired officer a second chance, indicating they should be allowed another opportunity after years of being a model citizen. After all, Chief Everington gave Davis a second chance after he was fired early in his career, and now he was the chief of police doing the same for a person he undoubtedly thought deserved another chance.

Meanwhile, corruption allegations continued to raddle the department. "Bathhouse" McDonald revealed that he paid $100,000 ($1.4 million in today's money) for protection from the police. It was through a grand jury investigation and not the police department that sixty-two policemen were identified as involved in the illegal liquor payoffs. As word spread of the easy pickings, more cops became involved and demanded part of the action. The police became so greedy that they bankrupted the crook.

With all the negative publicity focused on LAPD and Chief Davis, calls for his ouster grew louder and louder. The police commission (three of whom Porter had appointed) had heard enough. On October 31, 1929, the commission charged Davis with incompetence and neglect of duty. The fuming Davis denied all the charges and prepared to fight the case in court. Davis and others in the city thought his removal was politically motivated, allowing those who supported Porter to get one of his favorites in the chief's office. But the chief had civil service protection, which meant the police commission could only remove him if, after a formal trial, he was found guilty of either nonfeasance, misfeasance, or malfeasance. Commissioner Willard Thorpe warned Davis, "There is a new day in the Police Department. understand me?" He continued, "This board is executive head of the Police Department from A to Z...this commission is going to take part in everything of vital import." The commission then drafted a "book of regulations" to instruct the chief on his duties.

During the ensuing months, the commission diminished the chief's authority, especially regarding his ability to appoint or promote personnel. Commissioner

Edgar T. Wehn, a Porter appointee, was a member of the 1929 grand jury that had indicted numerous crooked vice cops. If a vote were to occur for his dismissal, the scales for removal were tilted to the firing of the chief. This, in essence, ended Davis's control of the LAPD.

Davis was not alone in his clash with the police commission. The chamber of commerce and the downtown business associations endorsed the chief, as did the *Los Angeles Times* through its owner, Harry Chandler. The paper reported the situation as:

> ...one of the nastiest and most offensive underworld conspiracies ever developed here or anywhere else. His accusers include the lowest and most depraved types of humankind. Prostitutes are among them. Men who exist on the earnings of prostitutes are among them: They include gamblers, dismissed and disgraced former police officers, and denizens of the underworld to whom truth and honor and fair play are not understandable terms. The fight on Davis is an ugly mixture of politics, criminal malice and personal animosity.

Support for Davis also came from notables such as August Vollmer, one of the most respected names in law enforcement and the formal chief of the LAPD:

From several sources I learn that various political groups are attacking the Chief of Police of Los Angeles and are making an effort to have him removed. This has been the practice in Los Angeles for many years and has contributed mightily to the demoralization of the police organization….The city of Los Angeles is now receiving a quality of police work vastly superior to any before received, and it behooves the people of Los Angeles to support this intelligent, energetic and honest official.

Despite receiving support from many inside and outside the department, Davis was removed as chief of police. He was offered a position as deputy chief in charge of traffic—or he could resign. Rather than relive those harrowing days from years earlier when he had been fired as a young patrolman, Davis agreed to the demotion. He cleaned out his office, perhaps realizing that with new mayors come new opportunities. This would not be the last of James E. Davis.

Chapter 14

Fight for Control of the City

"Who did it, Charlie?" The dying man just shook his head.
"You'd better tell us now while you can."
"I don't know. Ask Spencer—he knows."
"Spencer's dead, Charlie."

—Los Angeles Police Detective and Charles H. Crawford, Los Angeles Gangster

Charles H. Crawford was sitting at his desk at 6665 Sunset Boulevard, marveling at his newly installed alarm system. The mobster wanted and needed to feel secure. But he took no extra precautions for that day's appointment at his real estate office. Crawford had buttons scattered around his room that, once pushed, would alert his bodyguards, who would come charging into his office, guns in hand, looking to shoot anyone threatening their boss.

Just as the office clock ticked to 3 p.m., Lucille Fisher, Crawford's young receptionist, greeted a man in a double-breasted blue suit whom she later testified was "fair-complexioned, obviously an American." She had not seen him before but noted that her boss greeted the handsome man with a big smile. "How are you?" said Crawford. "How have you been? Come in." A little later, Herbert Spencer appeared. Spencer was an author and editor of a political weekly that Crawford supported. Here again, Fisher noted that Spencer seemed relaxed and was acting friendly.

At around 4 p.m., Spencer's wife called, so Fisher knocked on his door and went in with her message. "They were sitting there at ease, talking," she later testified. Spencer came out and spoke to his wife, explaining he would be home soon. Thirty minutes later, Fisher heard a chair scraped back, what sounded like a fist slamming a tabletop, and raised voices; then she listened to what sounded like a skirmish and two loud shots. Spencer staggered out of the office, reached the street, and collapsed on the sidewalk. A large pool of blood encircled his body.

A witness who owned a small photography business said he heard two shots and saw a man walking out the building's side door, buttoning the jacket of his blue double-breasted suit. Crawford was found on the floor with his finger inches from his alarm button and taken to the hospital.

At the hospital, Joe Taylor, the LAPD's chief of detectives, asked Crawford, "Who did it, Charlie?" The dying man just shook his head. "You'd better tell us now while you can."

"I don't know. Ask Spencer—he knows."

"Spencer's dead, Charlie."

Crawford had a faint smile as he closed his eyes. He died a short time later, never saying who shot him—a genuine gangster, not even exposing his killer.

The killing of Crawford was a big deal. Rumors began circulating that the underworld would "tear the city to pieces." District Attorney Buron Fitts predicted the killing would cost Mayor Porter and the LAPD's new chief, Roy Steckel (1929–1933), their jobs. None of this transpired, but Crawford's death changed the political and criminal environment in Los Angeles for years.

Before Crawford lived in LA, he had struck it rich in Seattle with his collection of dance halls and saloons that dispensed vice to the wishful miners during the Klondike gold rush. Crawford had fled when the city caught on to his criminal activity. Landing on his feet in Los Angeles, the crime lord had opened the Maple Bar. Here he catered to the rich and famous, including some judges and politicians, who used the bordello conveniently located upstairs. Always dressed in flamboyant suits and adorning himself with flashy jewelry, Crawford made himself known.

Having become a "reformed sinner," Crawford gained the city's attention after dropping his $3,500 ruby ring ($52,000 in today's money) in a church's collection plate.

He then gave $25,000 ($400,000) in cash to St. Paul's Presbyterian Church, run by his good friend Gustav Briegleb. The church used the gifts to erect a Parrish House in honor of Crawford's mother.

With the onset of Prohibition, Crawford saw enormous opportunities in the bootlegging industry. Looking for a lieutenant to run his day-to-day operations, he found gangster Albert Marco and expanded his vice operations with his prostitution houses throughout the city. In 1921, he became affiliated with Kent Parrot, who had just gotten George Cryer elected mayor. They struck up a business partnership that specialized in political corruption and vice. During the 1920s, they ruled Los Angeles and made millions.

Crawford's power abruptly declined during the 1929 mayoral race when he put all his bets on incumbent Mayor Cryer just as Parrot had pulled his support in favor of a challenger. Bypassing them all was John C. Porter, who was elected to head the city. With Cryer out, Crawford was again looking to claw his way to the top for control of the city. Standing in the way was Guy McAfee, a former policeman fired for running a craps game at a police station. During the 1920s, McAfee had worked for Crawford and married a woman who had run one of Marco's brothels. With Porter as mayor and Crawford losing his grip on power, McAfee was the chief rival of Crawford—and many would agree that he was a deadly rival. Crawford also financially supported Herbert Spencer and his magazine, *Critic of Critics,* which posed as a liberal reform voice for city members and had fifteen-thousand subscribers. Crawford directed Spencer to write several negative articles that named McAfee as the leader of LA's illegal casinos and vice operations, calling "Guy McAfee—the 'Capone' of LA." In another article, Spencer had written: "TO WHOM IT MAY CONCERN— A few days ago one Guy McAfee, who lords it over certain phases of the Los Angeles neither regions, informed a member of the staff of the *Critic of Critics* that unless this publication 'got wise to itself' he would see to it that we were 'taken apart.'"

The first twenty-four hours ticked by since Spencer and Crawford had been murdered, and no one had been arrested. The LAPD felt pressure to do something—quickly. Knowing the public animosity between Guy McAfee and Crawford, the LAPD arrested McAfee as the prime suspect in the double homicide. Although the arrest made headlines, it quickly fell apart when McAfee proved he had been downtown at the Hall of Justice when the shooting had occurred.

David H. Clark, a popular and handsome deputy district attorney and candidate for a spot on the municipal bench, suddenly confessed to the murders, which saved the LAPD further embarrassment. At just thirty-two, Clark was a climber in the justice system. His arrest shocked almost everyone in LA. As a policeman put him in handcuffs, Clark told police he wanted an immediate trial.

Around the city, it was widely known that Crawford and Spencer carried guns, although the police found no weapons at the murder scene. Clark told the police that Crawford intended to "get" Chief Roy Steckel. Clark told Crawford that the chief was his friend and would have nothing to do with his removal. Crawford became agitated and charged Clark, who fired one shot at him, putting him on the ground. Thinking Spencer was about to attack him, Clark fired another shot, killing him, and fled the scene. Clark later claimed he was innocent, as he had acted in self-defense. This was convenient as the two men who could refute Clark's statements were both dead. Later the police discovered that he had bought the murder weapon, a .38 caliber Colt with fifty copper-coated bullets, the day before the shooting. He had paid with a check that bounced.

Clark's boss, District Attorney Fitts, had previously raved about his deputy district attorney. Now he rapidly distanced himself. "There were three racketeers in that room," he said. "The murders were nothing more than the result of Crawford's attempts to regain the power he lost two years ago. Racketeers met racketeers, and there was murder." The DA made it clear he would seek the death penalty. Fitts assigned Clark's friend, Joseph Ford, as the special prosecutor. Once Clark and Ford were both in the courtroom, any hint of their friendship was gone, as Ford was determined to convict the former deputy district attorney. On Monday, August 3, 1930, the first day of the trial, a crowd fought with fifty bailiffs to get a seat in the tiny courtroom. Most were supporting Clark.

During the trial, Ford argued that Clark had the support of Guy McAfee to ensure Clark would get on the bench. Ford also put doubt in the jurors' minds, pointing out how Crawford, who had been out of shape and middle-aged, could not have attacked the athletic 32-year-old Clark. And Ford argued Clark was the only person with a gun in that small room. But the prosecution erred when they failed to produce a murder weapon or provide a motive for the killings. Clark changed the direction of the trial when he took the stand and produced the murder weapon, while his attorney built a strong case for his self-defense.

When it was over, the trial ended in a hung jury: eleven for acquittal and one for manslaughter. The jury was dismissed. Later, the juror who held out for a conviction had a bomb thrown at his house that failed to detonate. The DA refiled the case. A second jury found Clark innocent. Although Clark lost his election while on trial for murder, amazingly, he did receive sixty-seven thousand votes. Clark never recovered from the ordeal and, in 1953, shot and killed his friend's wife. He died in prison at the age of fifty-five.

With Crawford dead, Clark's Guy McAfee took over the reins of power, who was the conduit between city hall and the underworld. Mayor Porter also had his finger on the power button. Wrestling control of the police department from the police commission, of whom it was said he had signed letters of resignation as a condition of their employment. The mayor held this paper hatchet over their collective heads for their obedience. To ensure further control, Porter formed his own vice and investigative bureau. Leading the mayor's bureau was a disgraced detective, Deighton McDonald Jones, who Chief Davis had discharged because of his violent temper.

Additionally, the mayor forced Chief Steckel to move his headquarters from Central Station to City Hall. He also assigned the chief to an adjoining office. Porter went so far as to install a bell in Steckel's office and instructed the chief to respond when it rang.

In continued acts of control over the LAPD, and perhaps paranoia, Porter hired a group of amateur civilian investigators, who became known as the "Super Snoopers." Their assignment was to spy on the police commissioners, the police department, Chief Steckel, and even the mayor's own investigative vice bureau. These Super Snoopers, who had no formal police training, were issued LAPD captain badges. Their job was to sniff out vice and the corrupt cops who profited from it. Ultimately, the amateurs found little corruption because, according to the mayor, the cops "were too clever." The consequence of deploying these spies was the demoralization of the police force and the undermining of Chief Steckel's authority.

Yet despite the Super Snoopers' adverse effects, Porter would not stop spying. He directed the Super Snoopers' attention to city employees who disagreed with his religious interpretation. The Super Snoopers targeted Catholics and Jews, and many lost their jobs and pensions with little or no justification. When a veteran Catholic captain was fired for a minor incident just one year before receiving his pension, the LAPD leveled charges at the mayor for religious discrimination. Eventually, the captain was reinstated, but Porter's control continued unabated; he maintained a stranglehold on the department. Police cars were forced to carry political advertisements, and, under direct orders from Chief Steckel, officers had to campaign for city bond issues. At the same time, the chief hit the campaign trail in support of the man who had promoted him to chief.

On Good Friday of 1933, Mayor Porter went too far when he ordered the police department to stop all traffic in the city at precisely 3 p.m. because that was when, according to Porter, Jesus died on the cross. The resulting negative press hurt the mayor and ultimately destroyed his chance for reelection. That summer, Mayor Porter and his handpicked chief of police were out. Waiting in the wings was a patient James E. Davis.

Chapter 15

Second Edition

The Return of James E. Davis

"Those dirty low-down crooks on the homicide squad."

—Detective Jeremiah Hickey

He went by the name of Oscar Lund, alias George O. Hagen, alias Osigarty Lund. He was a busy crook. Between 1921 and 1934, he was caught thirty-four times while breaking the law. He committed nearly every crime listed in the penal code. His crimes included two murder charges, a few robberies, burglaries, counterfeiting, and vagrancy. Lund was on the LAPD's "Make Sheet," similar to the FBI's most wanted list. On July 6, 1933, the law again caught up with Lund when he was arrested on a murder warrant.

Per department procedure, the case was turned over to detectives from the elite homicide division. Two days later, the murder charges were dismissed. Land instead received a reduced charge of ADW (assault with a deadly weapon), and a few hours later, that charge was also dismissed. But under closer examination, the corruptness of the entire system stands out like a zebra amongst stallions.

Most criminals declare that it pays to have a good attorney. Lund did. A well-known LA lawyer Henry C. Huntington, with offices in the Civic Center, handled the case. A follow-up report on file with Lund's records signed by the detective states in caps: "INSUFFICIENT EVIDENCE TO SUBSTANTIATE MURDER CHARGE." The district attorney's office would not issue a complaint, so Lund was free again. That now made thirty-five times he had been arrested and yet was still walking the streets. Under a typical corrupt arrest, that would be the end of the story. But not this time with this man.

Shortly after Lund's release, and just as James E. Davis was being sworn in for the second time as chief, Attorney Huntington, in a drunken stupor, started bragging at his favorite cop bar about his success in getting Lund off a murder rap. Detective Jeremiah Hickey was listening. He was one of the good guys from LAPD homicide and had stopped by for a quick drink. Everyone in the detective bureau lovingly called him "Jerry." That was about to change.

It seems Huntington had mistaken Jerry for one of the men he dealt with from the homicide bureau and was bragging to him about how he had just passed out $2,500 (just under $50,000 in today's money) as a token of his appreciation for their "cooperation" in "springing" his client on the murder charge. Detective Hickey had been on the department since 1906, twenty-eight years, with an unblemished record despite being surrounded by some of the worst corruption in LAPD's history. Hickey was the detective in charge of the homicide squad, but this was the first he had heard of the $2,500 "deal." Hickey understood that conditions were sometimes "shady" within the bureau, but he was stunned to hear about Lund.

At work the next day, "loving Jerry" practically blew crime reports off desks when he thundered, "Those dirty low-down crooks on the homicide squad." As his words echoed through City Hall, he stormed towards the homicide detectives. Hickey screamed: "You can call me a 'stoolie' if you want to but I'm a tellin' you to your faces, I'm going right in and tell Chief Davis all about this whole rotten mess. You sons-of-bitches have gone around me just once too often." With that, he stomped from the room and headed to the chief of police's office.

Not long after, Chief Davis made headlines with a massive "shakeup" of the homicide squad, changes he thought necessary in his fight against corruption within the ranks. Two months later, Lund was arrested for counterfeiting. He was convicted and sentenced to six months in jail, the longest term available to the judge. That was arrest number thirty-six, and Lund was finally behind bars.

Corruption within the police department was just one black eye. The other shinner came from the mayor's office. In 1933, during the campaign to elect Frank L. Shaw, the term "reform" was, for the last time, used erroneously to improve a candidate's position with the voters. It was the same old story of City Hall cooperating with the criminal element for financial gain. Shaw was the last in a long line of unscrupulous mayors who had presided over the degradation of Los Angeles's municipal government. Corrupt elements within the police department followed suit. They took the agency to the brink of total collapse by the weight of "everyone is doing it, why should I miss out" corruption mentality. Feeding the nadir of the city and police force was the Great Depression tearing at the 'fabric of a once-thriving nation. Families were now simply trying to survive. Los Angeles had the highest personal bankruptcy rate in the country, and few could make ends meet. This financial distress was fertilizer for the growth of corruption in all aspects of city government.

Continuing with the customary corrupt mentality in LA, the newly elected mayor installed his own handpicked man in the chief's office, returning James E. Davis to lead the department—his second stint in the position. Since then, the name "Davis" and "corruption" have often been spoken in the same breath. The circumstances raise as many questions as answers.

Despite being labeled corrupt, Davis did not acquiesce to or condone dishonesty within his department and attempted to distance himself from a crooked City Hall. His actions were an exercise in futility. The chief was crushed by an entrenched, all-controlling political machine. And the engine powering this machine was the mayor's office. By city charter, the chief answered to the police commission. And the mayor controlled all appointments to the commission. He maintained this control by forcing the would-be commissioners to write letters of resignation before their appointments, like so many before him. If he needed leverage over a commissioner at any time, the mayor would threaten to use the resignation letter that was already signed, and his problem was resolved. Control of the commission gave him control over the chief of police.

Shaw, a former city councilman and county supervisor, quickly diminished the mayor's office when he hired his ruthless brother, retired Naval officer Joseph E. Shaw, as his secretary. "The Sailor," as he was known, set out to control all aspects of city government, looking to profit from it in any way possible. If a man wanted to be a cop, he was forced to pay up. It did not matter if a candidate was qualified when Joseph Shaw could sell appointments for $300 each. Promotions on the police department went to the highest bidders. Many disgraced officers bought their way back on the force and made graft the substance of their new positions.

While the old police commission from 1929 attempted to force Davis out of office, the new commission welcomed the new chief with open arms and assurances of a hands-off policy. The *Los Angeles Times,* which never waivered in support of the chief, wrote again in 1933.

> Prior to his undeserved demotion Davis established a record for personal honesty, courage, energy, and devotion to duty unsurpassed by any of this predecessors and under his direction the local police department was developing into one of the most effective law enforcing corps in the country. If given proper cooperation and support Chief Davis may logically be expected carry forward and to complete the work which he began then, and which has made little progress since his demotion.

After nearly four years on the sidelines in traffic enforcement, Davis returned to a department in the midst of a war—a war the department was losing. The endless press beatings and the outcry from the public demanding a safer city demoralized the police force. Politics and greed had torn apart the department from within. Ever-changing municipal administrations had elevated and eliminated police chiefs with discouraging regularity. Unscrupulous malcontents had been permitted to promote discord for their selfish interests.

There were weapons available to combat corruption within the police force, and Chief Davis was about to put them into play. First, he again stressed discipline. Second, he wished to increase morale by going after the minority of corrupt officers giving the department such an appalling reputation. The chief planned to eradicate corruption through unceasing, strenuous, fearless, and effective warfare against crime. Davis made it clear to the rank and file that he would investigate any form of corruption and dismiss offenders if warranted.

Chief Davis also examined a driving force of the city's crime: the influx of criminals from cold climates caused crime to spike in the winter. The criminals rationalized that if you are going to steal and plunder, why not do it in seventy-five-degree weather? Davis using information from his police statistician, knew crime was outpacing population growth. The numbers were staggering. In the past fiscal year under Stickel, there had been over ten-thousand burglaries and twenty-four hundred robberies, during which many of the suspects had been armed, and nearly eight-thousand vehicles stolen. With these astonishing figures, Davis made reviving his dragnet system his first official act. His strategy was to carry the war to the enemy and especially the gangsters from the East.

His plan called for a two-prong attack. First, Davis ordered street blockades in all major intersections for three consecutive nights from 7 p.m. to 1 a.m. Patrol officers stopped and searched any vehicle containing suspicious individuals. Police went through the cars looking for weapons or anything illegal. As a result of the blockades, most criminals were forced from the streets, seeking asylum in their hideouts, homes, or anywhere they could escape the pressure from the police. A dragnet immediately followed the blockades. In this operation, sections of the city were plotted on maps and divided into districts containing rooming houses, hotels, and apartment houses. Davis sent out squads of police officers, who went house to house, making inquiries and performing searches. They looked to catch suspected criminals who thought they could outwit the police by simply staying off the streets during the blockades.

The results were encouraging. Eighteen people, combined with 120 previous felony arrests, were arrested during the blockade's first phase. Six men arrested had been armed with revolvers; one man had a violent criminal record and had been charged fourteen times prior. Another suspect had been arrested for robbery. And four boys under eighteen were taken into custody for burglary.

Davis's dragnet also impacted major crime as it was happening. Robberies went from six to one. Burglaries went from twenty-nine to just fourteen, and thefts went from thirty-four to sixteen. Automobile theft dropped to a new all-time low of twelve. But while these numbers were positive, many law-abiding citizens who were stopped did not like it. They complained to the press and Davis. The chief replied that the police must have the citizen's cooperation if the dragnet was to work. He emphasized that if any officers were disrespectful, they would have to report directly to him. "The blockade speaks for itself when the results are studied," said Davis, who continued with the dragnet. He did so with the support of the American Bar Association, arguing that "citizens ought not to complain of slight delays and casual examination" by police.

Chapter 16

Righting a Wrong
Davis Leads a Fight for
Political Independence

"It has been an article of faith in Los Angeles politics for more than a quarter-century: Build the Police Department and its budget, and you build a stronger, safer city."

—*Los Angeles Times*

Since its founding in 1869, the LAPD has been mainly under the control of City Hall. Specifically, the mayor constraining the police. Throughout much of the LAPD's history, the chiefs of police had fought government politics more than it had fought criminals—not by choice, but for survival. By city charter, the chief answered to the police commission, which the Mayor controlled. Shaw controlled the department like puppets on strings. To contest this control and cut those strings, Davis formulated a plan. In early 1937, Davis understood that if there were to be a change in the status quo, it would have to be accomplished through the city charter. He planned to erect a ring of legal protection around his office, not unlike a castle's moat, that unethical politicians could not penetrate.

I believe Davis was a true reformer—something many historians disagree with. But the changes he sought illustrate my point. Davis paid officers bonus money during the Depression, and he lowered crime with his dragnets. The chief also created a bum blockade to stop criminal transients from entering the city. Furthermore, Davis reinstituted rules against officers accepting gratuities or soliciting rewards for doing their jobs. During his first three and half years as chief, he terminated 245 officers for misconduct. In a notable move, he recruited William H. Parker, a man who later became a saint to the officers in blue. No chief of police before or since has accomplished more for the LAPD than Parker did. Davis would not have put Parker in the office next to his if Davis were corrupt. Years later, people said Parker would have put his mother in jail if necessary—which was true. Parker was incorruptible, and Davis, understanding this, put him in his inner circle as his most trusted aid. Later Parker became Davis's best friend and hunting partner.

Lieutenant Parker was a rare individual. Working through school while a policeman, he obtained a law degree. Davis took Parker under his wing and made him his executive aid. He handled Davis's calendar and appointments and acted as the go-between with politicians and the commission. Parker served as the gatekeeper for Davis's office. Davis also sought his opinions. Both men agreed police officers faced a lack of job security.

By law, police officers were under civil service protection, but the chief and police commission could dismiss officers virtually at will. When officers were terminated, they lost their jobs and, in some cases, their pensions. For example, Captain John A. McCaleb was the hard-working commander of the Highland Park Division and the night chief. When he was charged with neglect of duty, conduct unbecoming an officer, and—the key phrase— "pernicious political activity," a panel from the department's upper echelons fired the twenty-two-year veteran. Everyone knew it was because he had refused to support Mayor Porter in his reelection bid. And, further, because he had worked to elect Porter's challenger, Frank Shaw. McCaleb was sacked. When Shaw won the election, his newly appointed police commission reinstated the captain. Through the Fire and Police Protective League union, Parker and another lawyer-cop, Earle Cooke, under the direction of Chief Davis, worked to amend City Charter 202 to offer fire and police officers added protection from direct political pressure.

In 1934, the city council permitted the league to place a charter amendment on the ballot that contained the key phrase to "clarify procedure in disciplinary and removal actions." Perhaps the council missed the fine print. The two police officers, educated as attorneys, sought a drastically expanded protection plan for police and fire personnel. Officers would have a one-year statute of limitations for charges to be brought. Officers would be allowed legal counsel at all hearings. They would be heard by a three-person rights board. The board would consist of captains or higher, with six names drawn randomly from a box. Of the six, the accused could pick three. The salient point of this proposed legislation was that the board's recommendations would be binding—no political interference. Only the chief of police could reduce the penalty but was not allowed to increase it.

Not everyone was excited to grant the police department the right to police themselves without outside influence. The proposal was presented to the voters as Amendment No. 12-A. On September 27, 1934, the amendment went before the voters and narrowly passed by just 676 votes: 84,143 in favor and 83,467 opposed. Chief Davis deserves recognition for selecting the right officers to push this legislation through.

Davis and Parker were men from different generations who met at opposite ends of their careers. Although they spoke with formalities in public, calling each other by lieutenant or chief in private, Davis and Parker became best friends. Together with their wives, they enjoyed the outdoors, hunting, and fishing.

In 1937 Davis applied Amendment No. 12-A to the chief's office. Davis had Parker go through the Fire and Police Protective League to draft an amendment to City Charter 1999. This was historic. If passed, the chief of police would have true civil service protection for the first time in the history of the Los Angeles Police Department. Protection from political interference coming from the mayor's office and many times directed through the mayor's appointed police commission. The ballot initiative was only one sentence but could fill volumes for what it was attempting to do:

> Shall proposed charter amendment No. #14-A, amending section 1999 of the Charter clarifying the civil service status of the Chief of Police, providing that he shall not be removed except for cause and

after hearing before the Board of Civil Service Commissioners, be ratified?

If the initiative passed, a chief could be suspended or fired only if found guilty of publicly stated charges after a "full, fair and impartial hearing." On April 6, 1937, Los Angeles voters sent a message to politicians everywhere when they approved Proposition No. 14-A by a solid margin: 79,336 to 69,380. The LAPD had come a long way from a bunch of officers gathered around a chalkboard looking to see if they still had a job after a new mayor had been elected. A chief was finally given legal protection for the first time and could not be removed from office at a mayor's whim.

Chapter 17

The "West Point" of Police Academies

"In Memorial James E. Davis. Through whose vision, leadership, and untiring efforts this police training and recreational training center was established."

—Brass plaque cornerstone at the LAPD Elysian Park Academy

During the depths of the Great Depression in 1934, Chief James E. Davis saw the need for a formal police academy. Davis wanted to educate the recruits, build strong bodies, teach marksmanship, and prepare each new officer for the tough streets of Los Angeles. Although Chief Vollmer had initiated officer training, there had never been a formal training academy. Instead, Lieutenant Ross McDonald was training officers at a "police school" in an old run-down armory. The other training venue was a shooting range consisting of two buildings in use since 1925. The double-decked (two-story) firing line had been built and used for the 1932 Olympic shooting competition, while the clubhouse had been an Olympic dining hall. These two buildings had few amenities and no plumbing or furnishings. People prepared meals on an outdoor fireplace, and an old-fashioned outhouse served its function. While it may not have been much, Davis consolidated the training school into the existing shooting range. He called it the Police Recreation and Training Center in Elysian Park, later naming it the Los Angeles Police Academy.

The idea of a police academy was sound, but raising the money during the Depression was difficult. Dollars were scarce, and because the city refused to finance the training center, Chief Davis persuaded officers to donate a portion of their minuscule Depression salaries to the cause. That money provided a solid fundraising foundation, but Davis needed more funds than the officers could realistically donate. So he went to Hollywood's massive movie industry. He invited icons to meals at the fledging academy. Guests included Cecil B. DeMille, his generation's Steven Spielberg, the young Shirley Temple, and other actors. Over lunch, the passionate chief explained his vision for training new police officers. Then the clincher: Chief Davis led them down to the shooting range, slapped a loaded gun in their hands, and taught them the basic fundamentals of marksmanship. As the starlets and movie moguls blasted away on the shooting range, a strange phenomenon occurred—the Hollywood royalty loved it. Generous donations for the academy's construction followed.

To raise additional funds for the training facility, the newly formed Los Angeles Police Revolver and Athletic Club published *The Guardian*, the department's historical annual. The extensive booklet was professionally produced, and Davis sold scores of personal advertisements, mostly paid for by actors and executives from the Hollywood movie industry. He also raised building funds through ticket sales to police shows held at the Coliseum. It was not unusual to have seventy-thousand police supporters in the stands. These citizens witnessed an elaborately choreographed performance, beginning with a parade of floats and ending with a three-ring circus.

Soon, the chief's creative fundraising efforts raised enough money to begin construction on the new academy. The trustees did all the labor for the academy's construction except for the gymnasium, which was a government Works Progress Administration project. Francois Scotti, an accomplished landscape artist, was commissioned to design and build the rock garden with four pools, several cascades, a small theater for band and stage settings, and an outdoor dining area. A large patio, barbecue pit, stairways, walks, and recessed stone seats also were included.

In August 1936, the first cadet class graduated from the Police Recreation and Training Center. In one of the LAPD's proudest moments, thirty-nine graduating cadets marched past the reviewing stand and saluted Chief Davis— the man who had the vision for the academy and saw it to fruition. To this day, every Los Angeles police officer marches across that field. Recruits such as Daryl Gates, Tom Reddin, Tom Bradley, and Michal Moore took those steps, as did thousands of other men and women who quietly had careers protecting and serving Los Angeles's citizens. According to Lieutenant Joe Dircks, the first academy range master, all the recognition should go to Davis:

> Chief Davis certainly deserves all the credit for building the Academy. While all these things were done in the name of the Revolver Club it must be remembered most if not all those who helped so much probably had never even heard of the Club, they did it because Davis had asked. Without the help of his friends the Academy would never have been built.

During their six-week course, the recruits engaged in marksmanship training. In a report to the mayor, Chief Davis noted his patrolmen's newly improved shooting abilities: "In the past two years, my patrolmen have killed thirty-eight criminals in gun battles and wounded 120 more." Joe Dircks recalled how Davis loved to put on shooting exhibitions for the public to demonstrate his officers' skills:

> So, I would be out with him [Davis] one or two nights a week and putting on these shooting exhibitions, when he was telling the audience how he taught the policemen to kill the villains. He would get a big hand for this.

These shooting exhibitions were a public relations mega-hit. Davis, who was a bit taciturn behind a podium, was in his element when he held a gun before the scores of on-lookers at his "Badge Day" luncheons at the academy. Starting during his first term as chief, Davis had given speeches to any group that invited him. He talked before Rotary, the Elks, local high schools, and women's organizations such as the Daughters of the American Revolution. He lectured against the evils of communism, the unions, and the transients that inundated Los Angeles in the winter, causing the crime rate to soar. He hated the gangsters and vice.

But not everyone agreed with the chief. One local newspaper labeled Davis a "burly, dictatorial, somewhat sadistic, bitterly anti-labor man who saw communist influence behind every telephone pole."

After Davis had lectured, the chief and Dircks would put on a two-man shooting exhibition with their portable bulletproof backdrop. Both men refined their demonstration into a Hollywood production, which the public loved. The chief still talked of communism's evils but added several new twists. After lunch at the academy cafeteria, the chief lined up his guests and handed each adult an LAPD detective-lieutenant badge. The smiling entourage followed him to the shooting range, where they saw a policeman standing about fifteen yards down range with a lit cigarette dangling from his mouth. Standing behind the shooting counter, with his gun at the ready, was a marksman, usually Lieutenant Dircks. As the guests fought to get the best view, Chief Davis hollered, "Raise pistol!" With this command, Dircks leveled his long-barreled .38 directly at the officer. A hush quickly consumed the crowd as guests anticipated being witness to mayhem. Just as Dircks was about to shoot, Chief Davis yelled out:

> No! Wait! Just a minute here, Lieutenant, wait just a minute. I'll hold that cigarette. In

the Los Angeles Police Department a superior officer never asks a man to do anything he would not do himself.

As Dircks lowered his pistol, Davis, in his pressed dress uniform, walked smartly to where the officer was standing. Placing a cigarette in his mouth, he dismissed the officer and bravely turned sideways to Dircks as if he were about to take one for the department. The crowd was tense. Decisively the command came from the policeman: "Raise pistol!—Fire!" The blast from the revolver shattered the stillness, and the bullet ripped the end of the cigarette cleanly off. There was silence as the crowd made sure the chief was still standing—then the crowd yelled and clapped for what they had just experienced. There was a collective feeling of relief in the air. The chief's mission was accomplished, as he had just transformed three dozen citizens into die-hard police supporters.

Chapter 18

The Bum Blockades

"Those vagrants do not come here to seek work but to go on relief, to beg or to enter into crime."

—Chief James E. Davis

Americans were having a tough time. The stock markets had failed; the Midwest had a disastrous drought, and the dry winds seemed to blow the dust and poverty toward California. Without Social Security, unemployment insurance, or federal welfare programs, two-million Americans were homeless by 1932, and 25 percent were unemployed. In one year alone, Southern Pacific Railroad guards threw nearly seven-hundred-thousand vagrants off its trains. As John Steinbeck wrote in *The Grapes of Wrath*, the travelers were from "Kansas, Oklahoma, Texas, New Mexico; from Nevada and Arkansas families, tribes, dusted out, tractored out. Carloads, caravans, homeless and hungry; twenty thousand and fifty thousand and a hundred thousand and two hundred thousand."

The Dust Bowl exodus was the largest migration in American history. It took place between 1930 to 1940.

Roughly 3.5 million people left the Plains states and headed to the West Coast. With the federal government distracted with other aspects of the Great Depression, individual states and some large cities, including Los Angles, responded to this mass influx of drifters.

Davis has taken considerable criticism for his style of policing and his views on constitutional rights. This criticism began with an article in the *Los Angeles Record* in 1929. Titled "Why Liberals Oppose Davis," the *Record* wrote: "It is an axiom with Davis that constitutional rights are of benefit to nobody but crooks and criminals, and that no perfectly law-abiding citizen ever has any cause to insist on 'constitutional rights.'" The paper continued, "Chief Davis honestly and sincerely believes that the whole country would be better off if the whole question of constitutional rights were forgotten, and everything left to the discretion of the police." The paper defined "liberals" as people who "believe in constitutional rights—to the point of insisting that no authority in the land—police, judicial or presidential—shall override the constitution-given rights of the meanest individual."

Chief Davis's proactive approach to policing was ahead of its time by nearly half a century. Fifty years after Davis instituted it, Chief Daryl Gates (1978-1992), developed a proactive policing method soon used by other larger departments, including NYPD. The approach included deterring criminal activity by showing a strong police presence and discovering offenses and conspiracies to commit crimes, thereby preventing crime from occurring in the first place. Davis' methods were very similar with his use of dragnets, rousting, and even the bum blockade (stopping transients from entering LA) to address serious crime problems actively. He utilized innovative police practices and policies that took a more proactive approach to reducing crime. It was a well-thought-out tactic based on a statistical analysis of crime problems and the areas where they occurred. Davis developed policing strategies intended to prevent and reduce crime in specific locations. Officers saturated the high-crime area and selectively stopped and interviewed suspicious individuals. Citizens going about their business could pass with little or no questions asked.

When some condemned Davis in the media, along with outspoken liberals, for violating the migrant's constitutional rights with the bum blockade, the chief clarified his interpretation of the issue:

> We are not interfering with American citizens, and we are not taking away their constitutional rights of ingress and egress across the borders of our States, but we are

protecting our citizens against enemies of society who roam about the country seeking green pastures in which to forage and who are not looking for gainful employment. It is true that citizens of the several States are citizens of the United States, free to roam about at will. The police department is not alone interested in the economic aspect of the migrant problem. We are primarily interested in finding criminals and stopping potential enemies of society from coming into our State and city and increasing our crime problems.

Some authors have suggested that Davis alone proposed the idea for the bum blockade, but that is not the case. In early 1936, the police commission contacted Mayor Shaw to suggest using the LAPD to reduce the number of indigents entering the city. Officials of border counties would need to deputize Los Angeles police officers, establishing their authority outside the city limits. Sheriff Eugene Biscailuz wanted nothing to do with this practice, questioning its legality. Mayor Shaw solved that problem in the short term by turning over the plan to the city attorney for a legal opinion. They came back and ruled it would be legal to use police funds for the stated purpose.

The city attorney had history on his side in making this ruling. The border patrol was one of several actions and legislative initiatives adopted by states to restrict migration during the Depression. Beginning in 1934, Florida had its own blockade for three years. In 1936, Colorado blockaded its southern borders against migrant beet pickers. In all, twenty-seven states established some form of anti-migratory laws. Davis's border patrol was not breaking new ground or purposely formed to violate people's constitutional rights through enforcement. Many of these transients were poor and became a burden to larger cities for their crimes and the need to care for them.

During the Depression, most cities could not afford the new financial burden and found it simpler to keep these transient people out of their towns. Some state legislatures made it a crime to bring migrants into the state and set up laws to deport them to outlying states. A billboard in Tulsa, Oklahoma, warned there were "NO JOBS in California" and for them to "KEEP Out." Los Angeles had problems with these migrants and took preventive measures to stop them.

After receiving the decision from the city attorney's office, Mayor Shaw made his position clear:

> It is important to note that Los Angeles is facing a desperate situation if we permit every incoming freight train to bring us a new shipment of unemployed, penniless vagrants to consume the relief so seriously

demanded by our own needy people and to create a crime menace almost beyond conceivable control. Our only recourse is to reinforce the sheriffs of the border counties of the State with men loaned from the Los Angeles Police Department, who can turn back the front ranks of those oncoming hordes promptly and in such numbers that the invasion will be halted at its sources as soon as the news reaches the East.

With orders from the mayor, Davis reverted to his proactive approach to solving the problem. In principle, he would build on his successful dragnet tactic. Davis dispatched 136 officers to the major points of entry along California's borders with Oregon, Nevada, Arizona, and numerous counties bordering LA, such as San Bernardino, Riverside, and Imperial. He assigned officers to sixteen critical highways and railroad crossings bordering the state lines.

The chief ran his plan through members of the Breakfast Club, the moneyed elite in LA. He explained that keeping the "thieves and thugs" out of Los Angeles would save $1.5 million and another $3 million in welfare payments. Davis described how he would direct his officers to stop the vagrants who came into the state by "stealing rides" on trains or hitchhiking. "Those vagrants do not come here to seek work but to go on relief, to beg or to enter into crime." He predicted the word would soon get out and echo across the country that people could not get into LA, thus impeding the flow of migrants. The officers were directed to ask two questions to the migrants: "Any money?" Any work?" If the answer was no, the wanderers were given a choice: thirty to eighty days of hard labor for vagrancy and nonpayment of train fare or to head back from where they came. All others could continue on their journey.

Speaking to the congregation of the Garvanza church, Davis quoted from the scripture to explain his plan.

> St. Luke quotes Jesus as saying that 'if the good man of the house had known what hour the thief would come, he would have watched, and not have suffered his house to be broken through.' The activities of your Police Department are based upon knowledge gleaned from past experiences. We are interested in striking at the criminal and his source and we are doing it in a legal, intelligent, and effective manner.

After two months of effective enforcement, LAPD border patrol officers returned to the city. Davis received many accolades for stemming the flow of migrants and lowering crime. "We hope your police will continue their good work," wrote Clarence Wearthan, manager of the Rocky Mountain Motorists Association. "It is time every community take such action as yours. You can rely upon our co-operation." Davis reported a 25 percent drop in major crimes and a new low in vagrancy and panhandling arrests as proof his dragnet on the border had worked. Davis' plan worked to perfection.

Chapter 19

The Red Squad

"Abolish the Red Squad."
—Communist protesters

"Order, order, order," yelled Los Angeles City Council President Charles Randall. He was furious at the John Reed Club for creating a disturbance in his chambers. These communists sought to expand their influence among radical and liberal intellectuals, screaming for justice from LAPD's Red Squad. Shouts to "Abolish the Red Squad" echoed through the large room. Events were quickly getting out of control. Randall was pounding his gavel so hard that the head flew off. Left with just the handle and his hand turning red from the repeated impact, the council president again demanded order. This time he was met with even louder screaming: "Abolish the Red Squad, abolish the Red Squad," the John Reed club members chanted.

Just out of sight of the protestors was the squad the communist wanted to be eliminated. Leading the squadron of officers was the man the council knew could be relied on to return order. Captain William "Red" Hynes was the man the communists wanted fired from the LAPD.

Hynes had encountered such protests before; that is what he did. So he bided his time, waiting with his men for the go-ahead he knew was coming. Abruptly, Randall screamed for the removal of the unruly protestors. Within seconds, Hynes and three of his largest officers charged the heart of the boisterous crowd with their fists, billy clubs, and blackjacks flying. Spectators there for other business scattered like sheep from a wolf as the wild brawl between the police and the communist took over the entire council chambers.

Hynes and his men forced the group out of the room and literally through a glass door, smashing it into shards. The police handcuffed three bloodied protestors and took them to jail. They called ambulances, transporting several people with bloody heads and broken limbs to the hospital. Two detectives made the same trip because they had broken bones in their hands.

After the disorder and before adjourning, the city council took time for a motion for members to thank Captain Hynes and his men for their "courage displayed in preserving order."

Hynes's nickname, "Red," didn't come from his hair, which was brown, but from his hatred of communists. A combat veteran from the Great War, he joined the LAPD in 1921. Within two years, he had received an assignment that would define him and the LAPD's disdain for radical labor unions and communists. Going undercover, Hynes had infiltrated the elite International Workers of the World (IWW) and the Communist Party. Working alone undercover, with no lifeline to the police department, is not a job many would seek or excel in, knowing if you are discovered, you will probably be killed. But for Hynes, he thrived. He became the secretary of the IWW strike committee and editor of its bulletin. Working in these influential positions, Hynes had gathered incriminating evidence against the key players within this group. In court, he had shown no emotion as he testified against the men he deceived.

A United States Justice Department official later singled him out for doing "more than any other person to help the federal government in their operation against the IWW throughout the nation during [their] general strike" and for "breaking up the IWW in Southern California."

From its inception in 1919, the Communist Party in the United States had been constantly under attack from city, state, and county law enforcement at the behest of the federal government. The administration believed communists threatened democracy as they encouraged revolution and worked to overthrow the U.S. government. During the first half of the twentieth century, communists were deeply rooted in American labor, civil rights, unions, and anti-war movements.

As with anything controversial, individuals and organizations take sides, exacerbated by everyone believing they are on the right side. Supporting the Red Squad were the Merchants and Manufacturers Association, the Better American Federation, certain metropolitan newspapers, and the Chamber of Commerce. Opposing the Red Squad were the libertarians whose perspective always had been peace, prosperity, and social harmony fostered by as much liberty as possible with as little government as necessary. The Los Angeles City Council supported Hynes and the Red Squad, as did the police commission. In one meeting, Commissioner Mark A. Pierce stated the police commission's position: "The more the police beat them up and wreck their headquarters, the better…Communists have no constitutional rights, and I won't listen to anyone who defends them." Red Hynes could not have been happier.

The business elite of Los Angeles ensured the city council, police commission, the press, and even the state legislature gave Hynes the support he needed. These captains of industry guaranteed that Hynes could publicly expose and discredit communists. Even the powerful county grand jury supported the Red Squad's actions. In 1931, the jury heard fifty cases involving the squad rupturing people's kidneys to breaking their bones. In one case, a burly policeman beat a photographer and publicly smashed his camera. The thrashing was so severe that several citizens stepped in to subdue the officer. After hearing testimony in all these cases, the grand jury ruled that there were a few uncivil officers but that criticism of the LAPD was "unjust and unmerited." Red Hynes acted as if he had the city in his back pocket—because he did.

An aspiring reporter, Jake Jacoby, was covering a campus protest for his college newspaper when the Red Squad showed up:

> The left-wing element at the college and the communists decided to hold a peace rally on campus so the college called for help. They sent out some big officers that were members of what they called Red Hynes Red Squad. They called on everyone to disperse but nobody did. This woman was still talking when one of the members of the squad hit this girl over the head with a sap.

When the communists sought parade permits, the paperwork went through Red's office, and most of the time, he denied these permits. When he could not deny the licenses, he had five-hundred policemen—a quarter of the department—as a backup. His tactics included getting within the ranks of the parade and shoving marchers until the march was disrupted, either because they fought back or the parade members dispersed. Red referred to these marches as "shove days."

Captain Hynes was also an expert at fighting with his declarations. Often, he would receive criticism from the press and would not hesitate to disparage the papers, complaining of "the damnable vilification and vicious attacks by [the] metropolitan dailies." He added that these attacks were "based on propaganda from Moscow." He especially went after the *Los Angeles Record's* denunciation of the Red Squad based on a policy of "glorification of avowed Communists, anarchists, criminals, and malcontents." Sometimes he accompanied Chief Davis and Lieutenant Dircks on shooting exhibitions. He would tell the assembled crowd to contact the press and have them "force the cessation of articles criticizing the police department." He also offered a handout depicting how the communists had formed octopus-like organizations whose tentacles reached virtually every street in Los Angeles.

When Shaw was elected mayor, he cut back on the Red Squad's activities. He opened a "free speech zone" at the Plaza that many communists took advantage of because it was a hands-off area. With his workload reduced, Captain Hynes took a leave of absence to serve as a consultant to various anti-communist groups. In 1938 Chief of Police David Davidson (1938–1939), in a massive department shake-up, transferred two-hundred officers, stripped Hynes of his rank as captain, and demoted him to a regular patrolman, assigning him to West Los Angeles Division. Hynes retired in 1943 with little fanfare.

Chapter 20

The Battle for Control
of the County Grand Jury

"Our auditors have discovered what appears to be some of the worst forms of graft and corruption that ever infested a body politic."

—Dr. John P. Buckley, Grand Jury Foreman

The political wars of the mid-1930s were mainly waged for control of the county grand jury. The jury's power to investigate municipal and county politics made it a battleground between reformers and the entrenched political machine, each attempting to maintain a majority panel of eight votes out of twelve, which was needed for an indictment. For decades, corrupt business elites and politicians controlled the grand jury. But when Fletcher Bowron, a superior court judge and later the mayor of Los Angeles, oversaw the 1934 jury, he altered the course of Los Angeles's corrupt history.

A local boy, Bowron had attended the University of California, Berkeley, and the University of Southern California Law School. Before becoming a lawyer, he had been a newspaper reporter and later served in World War I. While a police reporter for the *Record*, he learned about corrupt politics in Los Angeles and the police department. On the bench since 1926, Bowron witnessed a decade when the political and financial elite came to trial but managed to escape penalty through bribery—whether that bribery was of a judge, jury, or prosecutor. During the Depression in 1934, Bowron stood out as a reformer and became known to those Angelenos who fought for a clean city free from corruption.

Judge Bowron began the jury selection process by taking a month to interview scores of potential members for the grand jury. He used background information from his investigators to ensure the potential candidates met his requirements for a jury free from outside influences. Although we would not state publicly the type of jury he was forming, it soon became apparent that his interest was to end deep-seated vice, gambling, and political corruption. His instructions to the newly formed grand jury bore this out.

> The grand jury is particularly charged to exert its greatest and most conscientious efforts toward the securing for the people of this county clean, decent, and honest

government. There is no better field of endeavor for this grand jury than to search out graft or corruption or willful misconduct on the part of public officers, if any may be found. A dishonest and corrupt public official and all persons who attempt to bribe or corrupt public officials or public employees should be dealt with like any common or dangerous criminal.

As he formed the grand jury, attempts were made by corrupt city officials to block funding for investigative-related expenses. Without the funding, the grand jury could not do anything of substance. One gangster bragged, "We have the grand jury stopped. They'll never get a dime." The *Daily News* charged that James Bolger—the man forced upon Chief Davis as his "secretary" and who had been Mayor Shaw's campaign manager along with Sheriff Eugene Biscailuz—had arranged with the county supervisors to withhold funds. District Attorney Buron Fitts, who had a nest egg of $60,000 in a secret service fund traditionally shared with the grand jury, did not release a penny. Only through public donations did Bowron raise the necessary funds for the grand jury to function.

With funding, the grand jury was back to work. The associates probed street paving, lighting, and trash collection, which led to two former council members being indicted, as well as the general manager of the public works department. Dr. John P. Buckley, foreman pro tem of the county grand jury, reported: "Our auditors have discovered what appears to be some of the worst forms of graft and corruption that ever infested a body politic." The grand jury expanded their inquiry to the city and county for tons of paving mixture used in street repairs which the city paid an exorbitant amount. The same was true for garbage contracts, fuel oil purchases, and supply costs. Corrupt city officials were paid off by these companies to award them the contract knowing the city was paying twice the average amount.

Mossier M. Meyer, Superintendent of City Street Maintenance, was indicted by the grand jury on twenty-six counts of bribery, charging $19,355 for promoting a "unique mixed material" used in repairing city streets. Investigators discovered it was sub-standard at best. The grand jury also found that certain councilmen had demanded $10,000 to $50,000 for a city contract for "patented paving" that cost as much as $7.20 a ton compared to the standard $2.30 per ton for similar paving material. As some corrupt courts tried the cases, many of those charged eventually escaped conviction. Newspaper headlines listed scandal after scandal, and it appeared almost everyone in City Hall had had their hands out for a payoff.

A new scandal in the health department caught many by surprise. Mayor Shaw's health commissioners had hatched a plan to attract funds from major poultry dealers by eliminating the small guys through high fees for licensing. Commissioner S. "Sammy" Gach represented the administration in the "chicken deal," attempting to eliminate 80 percent of the poultry dealers. W.A. Schwartz of the Los Angeles Poultry Association stated that the operation called for $5,000 as a down payment and $500 per month delivered to the mayor's brother, Joe Shaw. The health commissioner would then allow the poultrymen to raise prices from two to four cents a pound, but only if they paid.

As one case of grand theft went to a jury, Deputy District Attorney S. Ernest Roll told the jury that if there were no convictions in the case, "Why, some morning, if these people are allowed to operate without restraint, we are going to wake up, and about ten floors of the City Hall tower are going to be missing." The jury came back deadlocked. One can imagine the jurors driving home, glancing out the corner of their eyes to see if City Hall was still intact.

Chapter 21

The Explosive End to Corruption

"Gosh, I'm living on borrowed time. They'll get me, sure!

—George Bruneman, bookmaker

George Lester "Les" Bruneman was an ambitious man. He made a living as a LA bookmaker, enforcer, and gambler going up against a crowded field of contenders. Some took offense, but the gangster was prepared. In case of trouble, Bruneman carried a .32-20-caliber handgun in his waist ban and a .25 auto in his hip pocket. In the underworld, he was both feared and hated. Many had beefs with him for encroaching into their territory. In the early 1920s, Bruneman had arrived in Los Angeles as a small-time racketeer but soon moved up with his "muscling-in tactics." Simply put, he broke bones and ended many a gangster's career. But he was unsatisfied with just a small part of the city; he wanted more.

Bruneman made his move on other gangster territories. His tactics were simple. He walked into a bookmaking establishment and announced he was taking over "or else," making sure everyone saw his gun. It worked on several occasions, but several intractable bookmakers pushed back. While gambling at the Surf Club, Bruneman was shot by two men but who failed to kill the resilient gangster.

After recovering from his wounds, Bruneman told an acquaintance, "Gosh, I'm living on borrowed time. They'll get me, sure, and it won't be any more that six weeks at most." He was right—but it was quicker than he thought. A few weeks later, he was eating at The Roost Café at 2700 Temple Street when two well-dressed men calmly walked into the café with a gun in each hand. Without uttering a word, they shot Bruneman twelve times. As he lay in an ever-growing pool of blood, fighting for his last breath, the assailants ran out the front door. Frank Greuzard, a café employee, followed and attempted to get the license number of their car. The professional killers saw Greuzard and shot him several times. The innocent man fell dead on the curb in front of the café. The gunmen got away.

At the time of Bruneman's murder in 1937, other events were put in motion that would shortly stop his type of criminal behavior and what reformers had struggled to achieve during the previous four decades. The Los Angeles city government would be profoundly and forever changed, and the LAPD would form the foundation that would shape the force into the elite professional department of today.

Throughout its early history, the LAPD had fought the same cycle of reform followed by corruption as other large metropolitan cities had. For decades, the political machine and the underworld had maintained almost total control over the city and law enforcement. In 1938, this battle ended in Los Angeles. The developments that finally brought this conflict to its conclusion reads like a complex mystery novel—complete with espionage, bombs, attempted murder, and a notable cast of characters.

The opening chapter began two years earlier when the mayor and chief of police asserted that organized crime and protected vice were almost nonexistent in the City of Angels. This recurring claim made by politicians and chiefs for generations was not believed for one moment by a local businessman, Clifford E. Clinton—a man who would have a profound and everlasting effect on the city and star in the real-life novel.

Clinton was a virtuous and moral man, and he was rich. He made his fortune with a popular trend in the 1930s—the cafeteria. His motto was "Dine Free Unless Delighted," He meant it. Clinton, the son of Salvation Army officers, despised alcohol. He made it his mission to help those less fortunate than himself. The impoverished population loved the cafeteria owner for his five-course meals of soup, salad, bread, Jell-O, and coffee, for which he charged just five cents.

In 1934, Clinton was introduced to the world of politics. He was appointed to a committee investigating the county hospital's food service negligence and corruption. The committee's investigation implicated the mayor's office and the man sitting behind the desk, Frank Shaw. From the beginning of his administration, Mayor Shaw had ensured that city contracts, including those selling food to the hospital, were awarded without competitive bidding. He paid individuals in city government to use his handpicked contractors. For his efforts, Shaw received kickbacks. Clinton's committee uncovered solid evidence that the mayor and his secretary, who happened to be his brother, Joe Shaw, had been bribing people.

Eager to uncover corruption in city government, Clinton strove for a position on the Los Angeles County

Grand Jury. Blocking his appointment was a system of judicial appointments that favored criminal interests. Every year, fifty superior court judges worked together to appoint nineteen people to the grand jury. Many of these judges had strong connections to the underworld and vice operations.

Consequently, the corrupt judges guaranteed that the balance of power in the jury always went in Mayor Shaw's favor. These judges ensured that at least ten appointments would vote as the mayor wanted. It was like a stacked deck of cards in a poker game with the outcome predetermined. Consequently, most county grand juries avoided uncovering any significant misconduct. Shaw was allowed to keep the status quo—keeping corruption as it was while his bank balance kept increasing.

In 1937, the cafeteria owner became one of the nineteen jurors thanks to an uncorrupted judge. While the jurors were settling into their new position, Clinton immediately pressed for an investigation into the mayor's claim that vice was almost nonexistent in LA. Predictably, the powerful jury foreman, one of the ten pro-Shaw appointees, refused. Not to be deterred, Clinton took the issue to the mayor. Without trepidation, Clinton asked Shaw to approve the investigation. Clinton had knowingly put Mayor Shaw in a tight spot. Denying Clinton's request would create the impression that Shaw was hiding the fact there was rampant vice in the city.

On the other hand, if Shaw allowed the investigation, there was no telling what the reformer might uncover. Shaw rolled the dice and allowed the investigation. He was betting that the political novice would not have the support of the grand jury's majority.

With the unrestricted approval of the mayor, Clinton assembled a group of like-minded citizens and created the Citizens Independent Vice Investigating Committee (CIVIC). As the investigation began to uncover open vice in the city and corruption in city hall, Shaw saw his gamble would lose and abruptly withdrew his support for Clinton. It was too late. Clinton and CIVIC had documented over six-hundred brothels, three-hundred gambling houses, eighteen-hundred bookie joints, and twenty-three thousand illegal slot machines operating around Los Angeles.

As Clinton turned in his investigative report, the jury foreman refused to accept it on fictional claims knowing he had the support of his boss, the mayor. This should have been the end of the investigation and the report, just as it had in years past. But no one anticipated Clinton's persistence. Working in the background, Clinton turned to someone he was sure would support him—a man who also wanted to shut down corruption and vice in the city. Superior Court Judge Fletcher Bowron understood just how corrupt the city was. He acquired this knowledge while on the bench and as a city newspaper reporter working the crime beat.

Bowron used his legal expertise to show Clinton how to fight back—by publishing a grand jury minority report. When a judge overseeing the county grand jury shut down Clinton's progress, Bowron superseded the judge and issued a prompt counter-ruling in Clinton's favor. With all obstacles removed, CIVIC swiftly printed and passed out thousands of copies of the "minority report" throughout Los Angeles. The report was devastating for the criminal world and those who supported it. It exposed that underworld profits were financing the campaigns of select city and county officials. And it showed that these local officials were protecting vice operators. The report said:

> A deplorable bad influence is being exerted over local government by a powerful, greedy, ruthless underworld political machine supplied with an abundance of funds from the growing profits from illicit operations.

CIVIC further declared:

> The three principal law enforcement agencies of the county, the district

attorney, the sheriff, and the chief of police of Los Angeles, work in complete harmony and never interfered with the activities of important figures in the underworld.

The criminal establishment swiftly responded. The grand jury foreman labeled Clinton an "out of control" egomaniac and charged the restaurant owner as "Public Enemy #1." He said Clinton was seeking headlines to promote himself and his restaurant.

The underworld and many in city hall went after Clinton. When he asked for a permit to operate a second restaurant, having already invested a large sum of money, he was refused for no relevant reason. Taxes on his primary restaurant suddenly rose astronomically without explanation. Patrons started complaining of "food poisoning," while others slipped and fell at the restaurant. Things got dire when a bomb exploded in Clinton's home. The investigating LAPD detectives gave the bombing a cursory look and asserted that Clinton dynamited his house to gain publicity. But what these corrupt detectives did not expect was a witness to come forward. This witness described seeing a vehicle speeding from the bombing in a vehicle that matched the description of LAPD's Intelligence Division.

There was more. A twice-fired LAPD cop with a dubious past, Harry Raymond, had been run out of Venice and San Diego as their chief of police. The former was for making several false arrests and being indicted by the grand jury for extortion. In 1937, Raymond worked as an investigator for Clinton and CIVIC. Raymond was valuable because he knew where the LAPD buried its skeletons, having buried a few himself.

While not an honorable cop, he was a determined detective with proven investigative skills. Like a bloodhound with its nose to the ground, Raymond could always catch the scent. He dug up incriminating connections between the underworld, the LAPD, and the mayor's office. But then, with the bone of corruption firmly between his teeth, Raymond made a potentially deadly decision. Instead of giving the bone of information to his employer, Clifford Clinton, he kept it and attempted to blackmail his former associates in the LAPD. It proved to be the wrong decision.

In one of the most bizarre events in the city's corrupt history occurred on January 14, 1938, when Harry Raymond walked from his Boyle Heights home into his detached garage. He got into his car, and as he stepped on the starter, he ignited a massive bomb, setting off an explosion that shattered windows blocks away, destroyed his garage, and drove more than 150 metal, wood, and glass fragments into his body. Incredibly, Raymond survived the assassination. Lying in the emergency room, and most thought his death bed, Raymond managed to whisper to investigators that he suspected Earle Kynette, the LAPD's Intelligence Division commander, was the would-be assassin. With those words, a second explosion occurred as the lid of corruption was blown off LA.

Captain Kynette is perhaps the most infamous dirty cop from a long list of contenders. He joined the department in 1925 and quickly became the bagman of vice boss Albert Marco. Two years later, a police trial board found him guilty of extorting money from prostitutes and fired him. But the wily Kynette got reinstated and promoted to sergeant, most likely at the mayor's behest. When Marco had been sent to prison, Kynette had found new corrupt freedom under Mayor Shaw, out of whose office he worked.

Chief Davis, at a pistol match in Mexico, was unaware of the details of the bombing or who the suspects were. Kynette called the chief and told him of the bombing but did not tell Davis that he was a suspect in the case, something police officials had just told him. The chief ordered him to lead the investigation into the bombing. Ten days later, Davis arrived back in Los Angeles. The chief of police was briefed by Assistant Chief Roy Allen, who had command of the department while Davis was in Mexico. He told Davis that there was not enough evidence to charge any of the officers from the Intelligence Division. Based on this information and from other investigators in the bombing, Davis made a statement to the press:

> After a thorough and complete investigation of all angles of the case, I am satisfied beyond a doubt that no member of the Police Department had anything to do with the bombing of Harry Raymond. Keynett's surveillance of Raymond was a routine matter prompted by knowledge of the latter's acts in connection with groups which are antagonistic to the city government. That is part of the intelligence unit's work – to investigate such groups just as it is part of government intelligence units to investigate groups inimical to the government of the nation.

Critics of Davis and Mayor Shaw would argue that this statement to the *Los Angeles Times* supports the argument that Shaw and Davis worked in unison. They used Kynette and the Intelligence Division to obstruct any group or person they perceived as a threat. On the contrary, Davis made the press release on information he received from his second in command, who told him that Kynette was innocent, as was his entire unit. If your trusted deputy chief tells you "abc," you, as the chief who helped put him in that position, will quote "abc" to the press. Davis did not have time to investigate the bombing; he could only rely on his subordinates, who, for whatever reasons, exonerated Kynette. When Kynette and others were charged with attempted murder, they were immediately fired. Davis did his job as chief of police independently of the mayor.

A month after Raymond's attempted murder, a new county grand jury indicted Earle Kynette and two members of his Intelligence Division for the bombing. The following month, the criminal trial began. The testimony highlighted how Kynette and his cronies acted as amateurs in planning to get Raymond. Witnesses testified how Intelligence Division members climbed telephone poles to tap Raymond's phone lines. They even rented a home across the street as a command post to spy on the CIVIC detective.

One night, while the suspects had been sneaking around Raymond's house, a neighbor, George Sakalis, confronted the men and told them to leave. A few days later, he was beaten, robbed, and told to "keep your mouth shut." During the trial, Sakalis bravely pointed out Kynette and another police defendant as the men he had seen in Raymond's garage the night before the bombing. He further identified them as the two men who had assaulted him. Further evidence substantiated that Kynette had purchased the steel pipe used in the bombing.

Chief Davis took the stand to answer questions about the Intelligence Division and its commander, Kynette. His testimony revealed that the squad spied on county supervisors, judges, newspaper publishers, and others. He stated that if any of these people had criminal records, they were fair game for the unit to spy on, adding that some of those the squad observed had contact with "subversive elements." Davis stated he did not order the unit to rent the house they used to snoop on Raymond, and he did not know the squad had been spying on Raymond until after the bombing. It should be noted there was substantial evidence to back up the chief's claims of noninvolvement and indicate that Davis was not in the loop concerning this crime. Testimony established that Kynette and his Intelligence Division worked out of the mayor's office. Kynette's second in command testified that Kynette reported directly to The Sailor, Joe Shaw, which meant he bypassed the chief of police. None of the defendants pointed the finger of guilt at Chief Davis, which would have been easy to do.

The trial did not establish a criminal connection between the defendants and Davis. Although he had done an abysmal job handling the initial investigation, Davis was not culpable for the bombing of Raymond's car.

Kynette was convicted of three felony charges, including attempted murder. He received ten years in prison, as did Officer Roy J. Allen, who died of a heart attack in 1942 while serving his sentence in San Quentin. Kynette was paroled in 1948 over Raymond's protests. The former captain was then sent back to San Quentin in 1951 for violating his parole after he was convicted of being drunk. Freed again one year later, he got a pharmacist's license and worked in Twain Harte, California, when he was charged with drunk driving in a car accident that killed two people. Kynette beat the charge and died in 1970 at the age of 76.

The bombing had done more than fill Raymond's body with shrapnel—it instead solidified public opinion that the city needed to be cleaned up, and Mayor Shaw recalled. The reformers of LA came together to support Bowron, the judge who had earlier helped Clinton publish his minority report. After being recalled, Shaw ran against Bowron for mayor in 1938. Bowron soundly defeated him by running a well-financed and well-organized campaign, arguing that he would continue to rid the city of vice and corruption.

As for Joe Shaw, the mayor's brother, when indicted in court, he cried into his handkerchief, "I am a poor man…I've always been an honorable one…If this jury indicts me, I hope it won't make the bail too high." They did indict him, and Joe Shaw was convicted of sixty-six counts of selling city jobs and promotions. A year later, his sentence was reversed by the California Supreme Court, and The Sailor was a free man.

Bowron, the new mayor, made it clear there would be no place for Davis in his administration. The chief countered that he had done nothing wrong and would fight to stay on as head of the LAPD. To prove his sincerity, Davis disbanded the Intelligence Division, reassigned more than forty-eight officers, and renewed his attack on vice. The persistent chief gave up his battle only after his friend and executive officer, Bill Parker, suggested he could lose his pension if he continued to fight to remain as chief. Twice the department's chief of police, Davis, retired from the LAPD. As the *Los Angeles Times* stated:

> Chief Davis is not quitting under fire. His record is clean and in voluntarily closing it he has nothing to regret, to alibi for or to defend. Twenty-six years in the Police Department, during which period he has risen from its lowest to its highest rank and has seen the department's responsibilities grow in proportion to the city's own fivefold increase, is a record that speaks for itself.

History has not been sympathetic to Davis. Writers who have examined LAPD's past toss Davis in with the pool of corrupt officials from the 1930s. I disagree. It's essential to explore what Davis accomplished during one of the most tumultuous eras in American history. The man who arrived in Los Angeles in 1911 wearing an Army uniform retired in 1938, proud of his achievements. Davis did more for the LAPD during those intervening years than nearly any other chief in its history. He declared war on the Eastern gangsters and was able to claim victory. Davis slammed the door on the fingers of mayors and bureaucrats trying to control the department when he succeeded in getting a city charter passed that gave protection to the chief's office and the rank and file. This charter was an enormous legislative win that protected the department's integrity from the corruption that comes when politicians, such as the mayor, have absolute control over the chief of police.

Davis, through his aggressive, proactive policing, reduced crime during the height of the Great Depression. At the time, few law enforcement agencies in the United States equaled his success. Davis opened the department's first shooting range and, in his crowning achievement, used his unwavering determination to raise money for and build the

"West Point" of police academies. The Los Angeles Police Academy is, to this day, one of the finest police training programs in the world and has produced generations of men and women skilled in and dedicated to protecting their city.

While Davis' detractors will point to his handling of subversive organizations with the Red Squad and bum blockade as failures, the reality is that Chief Davis was following specific directives from the mayor and was successful in doing exactly as he was directed. Perhaps the chief's salient failure was his stalwart commitment to fulfilling his orders as he executed these assignments only to be second-guessed later.

Davis' contemporaries defended the chief against claims he was corrupt. They argued he was incorruptible and had led the LAPD to new heights. Two of LA's finest chiefs were among those who defended Davis. One was Chief August Vollmer, who strongly supported Davis in the late 1920s. The other was Chief William H. Parker, who defended Davis in the 1960s. Both men agreed Davis was an excellent chief and innovator.

The legacy of Chief James E. Davis should be given the same level of veneration and accolades as other chiefs who have taken the LAPD to new levels of professionalism. His name should be recorded along with the elite LAPD leaders such as Glass, Vollmer, and Parker. Taken in its entirety, Davis' career moved the Los Angeles Police Department forward, paving the way for the next generation to build upon.

From the turmoil of the 1930s, a new LAPD emerged and began to take shape. Never again would the department suffer from significant corruption within its ranks. Finally, the cycle of reform and corruption had been broken. A new era was just over the horizon.

Chapter 22

New Beginnings
The Shields

"You're cops, you're damned good ones. When you walk down the street, I want to see those chests out a mile, those heads carried high, and be damned proud when someone says, 'There goes an LA cop.'"

—William A. Worton, Chief of Police

With new leadership in the LAPD and the mayor's office, 1940 dawned like a spectacular sunrise, ushering in a new day of hope and promise. Leading in the new decade and new beginnings for the department was the first recruit class in three years and the first since the corrupt days of the 1930s. For these survivors of the Great Depression, 1940 brought visions of the good life.

The LAPD class of 1940 began with a revitalized merit system. These officers were not forced to buy their appointments; they earned them. Over six-thousand people applied for only seventy-eight positions. Those select few who became part of this class named themselves the "Shields" in honor of the newly copyrighted badge they would soon pin on their chests and is still worn by today's LAPD. History would prove these men worthy of these badges. The Shields turned out more chiefs and command officers than any other class in the LAPD's history. They were the new Los Angeles Police Department.

As these recruits jogged in a tight military formation through the hills of Elysian Park surrounding the police academy, they were led by a track star from UCLA named Tom Bradley—an officer who would one day become mayor of Los Angeles. Following close behind was Edward Davis (1969-1978), who would become chief two decades later. The Shields were the first class to benefit from improved training and instruction. One teacher was destined for LAPD greatness: Lieutenant William H. Parker. An attorney, Parker was the former assistant to Chief Davis. He had written the changes to Charter Section 202 that gave civil service protection to the chief's office. Parker was already a legend within the LAPD. Davis recalled Parker lecturing at the academy:

> I remember one thing about Bill Parker:
> He had great integrity. In my recruit class,
> the Shields, they sent a young Bill Parker
> to the academy, and he waved the bars of

San Quentin at you. 'If you get out of the line, you will wind up behind bars in prison; we will put you there.'

John Powers was one of the attentive recruits who listened to Parker. Powers would become the epitome of what a police officer should be. The young Powers had wanted to be a police officer for as long as he could remember. His ambition came from the cop genes flowing through his body. His father served thirty-six years as a policeman, and his grandfather did for twenty-one years. Powers himself would have a thirty-one-year career. He was a police professional who set high standards for himself and those around him. He understood the war against the criminal element:

> The police are engaged in a hot war. There are no truces, and there is no hope of an armistice. The enemy abides by no rules of civilized warfare. The individual officer, when taking his oath of office, enters a sacred trust to protect his community to the best of his ability, laying down his life if necessary. All men return to dust.

The Shields were indeed the new LAPD. Gone was the raw, two-fisted, hard-hitting tough cop of the previous generations. The new officers looked more like businessmen than the rigid cops of the early newsreels. This generation was better educated, socially conscious, and amiable toward the public. With Parker at the helm, these recruits formed a foundation of leadership that lasted into the 1970s and beyond.

Despite the honor, courage, and prestige the Shields brought to the LAPD, the department and the city it was sworn to protect were still struggling to maintain some self-respect among their leaders. The city's mayor had just been recalled; two LAPD officers had been sent to prison, and the chief of police had stepped down.

In 1939, newly elected Fletcher Bowron walked into municipal pandemonium when he entered the mayor's office. Graft and political patronage had been the rule for decades and were entrenched in all aspects of the city that it seemed they never would go away. Mayor Bowron accepted the challenge and made reform of the city his primary goal.

While the LAPD made substantial progress in becoming a professional force, the department still struggled. Progressivism as a movement ended during Bowron's long tenure in the mayor's office (1938–1953). Many of the old progressives died; others were voted out of office, and some retired. As the progressives left, so did the organized vice entrepreneurs, corrupt politicians, and crooked policemen. Bowron could not eradicate corruption wholly and instantly, but in his fifteen-year tenure, he kept criminals and crooked politicians in check.

With a large broom of reform, Bowron began the enormous task of sweeping the city clean. Civil Service Commissioner William Cormack and Joe Shaw were convicted of sixty-six offenses concerning selling jobs and promotions under the Shaw administration. Another man, Lieutenant Pedro Del Gado, who'd also been involved in selling police appointments, fled to Mexico to avoid prosecution. The mayor swept nearly one-hundred commissioners, including the entire police commission, into the trash. The new police commissioners were given three relevant policies to enforce: purging every aspect of vice, no matter how inconsequential; strict enforcement of police rules for proper conduct; and, most importantly, eliminating every officer deemed unacceptable because of their past actions. For the first time in decades, the new police commissioners were not required to submit their resignation letters upon appointment and were given the autonomy to do their jobs.

Bowron's abhorrence of vice was drilled into each commissioner. Commissioner Reverend John Kingsley proposed that unescorted women and women clad in slacks, whether escorted or not, be denied entry to nightclubs and bars. The relatively new escort services related to massage parlors were restricted to single-sex service and required attendants to be the same sex as their customers.

Next on the commissioner's list was to borrow Bowron's broom to clean house of the police force. They did so on March 3, 1939, citing City Charter section 181, which allowed the police commission to retire anyone eligible for pension "for the good of the service." The commissioners forced twenty-three high-ranking command officers to retire—a virtual who's who of the police department. These men had been flagged as possibly being untrustworthy or as having had knowledge of "deals and payoffs" from the 1930s and having failed to take appropriate action. Forced into retirement: former Chief of Police Roy Steckel; the Chief of Detectives Joe Taylor; an assistant chief; eleven captains; and nine lieutenants. Nine more high-ranking officers followed a short time later. The rank and file were not exempt from the purge. The commissioner interviewed police officers about their alleged breaches of regulations.

Over the next two years, the LAPD forced approximately 150 officers from the department. These men mainly chose to retire rather than lose their valuable pensions. Getting rid of corrupt officers, regardless of rank, was an essential first step toward reforming and professionalizing the police department. The LAPD made significant strides to maintain this momentum, but not without struggle and occasional defeat. The days of scandal and dishonor did not wholly fade away, no matter who was leading.

Purging so many high-ranking executives was profound because these men had cooperated with corrupt factions within City Hall and the underworld. Removing the crooked cop broke the syndicate's power and control of the city. It was an enormous step toward long-term reform. Gangsters saw the change, and most moved on. Guy McAfee had enough with the new LA and hightailed it to Las Vegas, where he opened a legal casino. Other underworld figures like Farmer Page moved out of the city and onto gambling boats in the harbor, while others left the City of Angels far behind. It was an amazing transformation.

As he took office, Mayor Bowron directed Chief Davis, before his retirement one month later, to provide a list of the 7,843 honorary police badges issued to Angelenos and get them all returned to the city. Bowron wanted them back because the owners could use them to get out of tickets or misdemeanors. Bowron was determined to put a stop to this decades-long form of corruption. The badges were handed out to citizens from all walks of life. There were movie celebrities like Louis B. Mayer, Clark Gable, Shirley Temple, bankers, wrestlers, brokers, painters, artists, brewers, judges, politicians, attorneys, and even ordinary day laborers. Clifford Clinton had one, even the Maharaja of India.

To continue cleaning up the city, Mayor Bowron needed a new chief of police who would share in his vision for the future. Preventing him was the new city charter that prohibited him from selecting the chief. Consequently, a civil service announcement went out to all LAPD veterans with a minimum sergeant rank and at least ten years of service. One hundred and seventy-one candidates took the written exam, hoping to be the new chief of police. Bowron was pushing for Captain R. R. McDonald, an FBI academy graduate, and friend of J. Edgar Hoover. Instead, out of nowhere, a little-known lieutenant, Arthur H. Hohmann (1939-1941), scored 98 percent, a whopping fourteen points higher than his nearest competitor, a deputy chief. Hohmann's score left the police commission in a dilemma. Should the members promote an unknown lieutenant to chief, bypassing several accomplished veteran deputy and assistant chiefs? The mayor weighed in and made it clear he did not want some anonymous lieutenant heading the LAPD.

After three tense weeks of controversy, the independent police commission, following the city charter, appointed Hohmann as chief. Hohmann's score was so much higher than anyone else's that it left the commissioners with little choice. Despite their hesitancy, Hohmann brought several essential qualities as the new manager: an unblemished record, which included his service during the Shaw years; unquestioned integrity; and unwavering moral principles. Mayor Bowron had a convenient change of heart. He announced that the mayor's office no longer would meddle in police department affairs: "There will be no attempt to control the police department from the mayor's office, no appointments will be dictated, and no transfers urged." The mayor came out in support of now Chief of Police Arthur Hohmann.

Born and raised in Northern California, Hohmann experienced the harsh realities of life when he was ten. Jolted out of bed by the great San Francisco earthquake, young Hohmann escaped outside only to witness the horror of his family's home burning to the ground. Later, the boy would watch as wagons hauled the earthquake victims' charred bodies to the city morgue.

Hohmann had begun his education humbly, attending a one-room schoolhouse in Hayward, California. Instruction ended after the eighth grade, so Hohmann had gone to work driving a team of horses for a cement factory but lost interest quickly. Hohmann became parched with an endless thirst for knowledge—a characteristic he maintained throughout his life. The future chief of police enrolled in a correspondence course to obtain a high school diploma. Having impressed his mail-order teacher, Hohmann had been able to enroll in a local high school and graduate when he was twenty-one. Soon after, in 1917, Hohmann enlisted in the United States Army.

The Great World War had exploded upon the scene. Although Private Hohmann had yearned to fight in Europe, he was relegated to "fight the battle of Texas," where the Army had built a new fort. Hohmann had studied relentlessly, achieved the rank of lieutenant, and was rewarded with an assignment to military intelligence. At the war's end, he was aboard a ship assigned to maintain cargo security. While ferrying back and forth across the Atlantic in an old coal-burning four-stacker, Hohmann had met an LAPD officer on leave from the department. This chance meeting changed Hohmann's life.

The stories he heard about a career in LAPD left an indelible dream that would come to fruition six years later. After coming ashore and bouncing around California, the twenty-nine-year-old Hohmann applied to become an LAPD officer in 1925. He was one of 160 recruits in the third class of the Police Training School initiated by Chief August Vollmer. Ninety days later, Hohmann was walking a foot beat with a senior officer. In 1983, I interviewed Hohmann about those days on patrol sixty years ago. The old chief began to laugh:

> You know, working a foot beat is the easiest and best job on the department. I think one of the most interesting calls I had was a family disturbance. I remember walking into a second-floor apartment and saw this guy with a knife to his wife's throat in a corner of the room. I quickly saw that the husband was full of hop. I also realized that I was a common enemy to both of them. I grabbed a kitchen chair [just as] the man swung. The blade stuck in the seat of the chair. I bet we went 30 minutes saying, "Yes, I will; no I won't [drop the knife]," until the man fell down drunk.

The new chief, the city's thirty-ninth chief in sixty years, immediately got to work scrubbing corruption from the department. He began by abolishing acting ranks, or "scabs," as he called them. Previously, it had been established to promote favorites to a higher rank, even if these officers had never taken the civil service test. Simply put, the "good ol' boys" rewarded those loyal to the givers. In one notable day, the new chief abolished 398 acting police department positions and promoted, demoted, or transferred nearly five-hundred other officers. By cutting out the scabs, Hohmann hoped to allow promotional opportunities for the many qualified officers previously denied advancement.

Hohmann restructured the city's fourteen patrol divisions into six, patterned after a military management style. He abolished the city's vice squad, forming a task force of eighteen men who monitored the city, ferreting out gambling and other vice activities. The chief liked nothing better than to accompany his troops on these raids.

The same man who, in the early 1930s, as a lieutenant, had drawn up the department's first manual of operations replaced fourteen divisional captains with three hand-picked men, two of whom had finished just behind him in the examination for chief. He further planned to rotate all department personnel every ninety days to prevent graft from flourishing. Although set in his ways and a strict disciplinarian, he was admired by his officers—not unlike Daryl Gates years later.

Although Mayor Bowron adjusted to Hohmann's management style, their working relationship was soon put to the test. Hohmann was a stickler for discipline, demanding things be done according to the book. However, Bowron wanted things done his way—no exception, and he did not care about book procedures. Bowron insisted that 170 corrupt policemen were still on the job and were a constant threat to the department. Circumventing the chief, the mayor hired a Chicago investigator to probe the city. According to a grand jury transcript, the investigator, Wallace N. Jamie, had tapped telephones and illegally recorded conversations between officers. Bowron put Jamie on Hohmann's payroll, and the chief made it clear publicly that he did not appreciate it. The mayor told him to eliminate the 170 corrupt officers—or else. Hohmann said no, as he did not have any evidence that would support firing these men. Hohmann told the mayor he doubted there was any proof.

Additionally, the chief pointed out that a statute of limitations—twelve months—came into play. If any illegal activity occurred before these twelve months, the officers were protected by civil service regulations. Because tapping phone lines was unlawful and could not be used in administrative hearings, and no proof ever surfaced about these men's guilt, Hohmann refused to terminate anyone. Bowron was furious. Immediately, this became a test of the new city charter that protected the chief of police. In years past, when the mayor had been displeased with his chief of police, the chief would soon be shown the exit. But with the new charter protecting the chief, there was little the mayor could do. Mayor Bowron remained infuriated.

Despite receiving the mayor's wrath, Hohmann continued to move his reforms forward and did a remarkable job leading the department. Chief Thomas Reddin (1967–1969) knew Hohmann well and stated, "Hohmann did too much too fast, but he was the first chief to turn the department around. He is tantamount to Chief Parker."

The mayor continued his pressure for Hohmann to relinquish his position as chief of police. Finally, Hohmann had enough. He resigned and accepted a demotion to deputy chief. To this day, people have speculated as to why Hohmann resigned.

Some attribute his resignation to the North American Aviation labor strike and riot. In this widely reported case, Chief Hohmann broke tradition when he failed to support management in the strike and instead remained neutral, simply trying to keep the peace. Later, the strike turned violent, and city officials called in the United States Army. The press blamed the chief for not taking action against the strikers. Others speculated that Hohmann's standoffish relationship with the politicians led to his self-demotion. As Hohmann put it: "The other chiefs hung out around the mayor, the city council, and police commissioners' office. I never did." When speaking to me in 1983, Hohmann explained why he stepped down as chief of police. He recalled a meeting with Bowron in which the mayor repeated his earlier allegation of corrupt cops:

> We are not happy…You are not cleaning the department of the crooks we think are out there. We think there are 175 crooks on the department, and you're not finding them. We want someone [as chief] who will find them.

Hohmann said somberly:

> Well, we lost our son that year [the chief's son died in a freak home accident, and his mother passed in the same week], so I said fine. He [the mayor] said, "You're number one on the deputy chief's list, so we'll designate you as deputy chief." I said fine. Then the next thing I know, my six-month probation period was two weeks from being completed when they terminated my probation, presumably for cause [and demoted Hohmann from deputy chief

> back to lieutenant]. Well, they have to
> show cause. Chief Horrall said I lacked
> managerial ability.

The chief was unceremoniously demoted to the rank of lieutenant and put out to pasture at the Highland Park Division. An attorney, Hohmann, used his knowledge of the law to contest the action. The Superior Court of California agreed the demotion was unjust and restored Hohmann to deputy chief. Hohmann received restitution of all back salary plus 7 percent interest. Hohmann laughed at the fact that he had made more money from the settlement than if he had retained his rank as deputy chief. After Hohmann won his court case, the LAPD brass got some revenge by assigning Hohmann administrative duty, with no subordinates and no one to command. Tucked away in an obscure office, Hohmann came to the attention of several council members, who noticed that every time they walked past his office, the deputy chief had his feet on the desk, appearing as though he had nothing to do. Under pressure from the council, Chief Clarence Horrall (1941-1949) assigned Hohmann to civil defense duties—another do-nothing job for the ex-chief.

At the end of World War II, Hohmann had been repeatedly given non-descript assignments until he retired in 1960. Even though civil-service protections were in place, the mayor and the City Hall bureaucrats had not forgotten how to wear down a chief. Hohmann retired to be with his children in Cool, California. He died in 1985 at eighty-nine from a car accident.

In June 1941, Mayor Bowron won reelection, and Hohmann was replaced by C.B. "Jack" Horrall. The forty-six-year-old Horrall, who'd grown up in Indiana, had been an infantry lieutenant during World War I and joined the LAPD in 1923. With a Bachelor of Science degree, Horrall separated himself from most in the department and scored 99 percent on the civil service examination. Horrall stated: "I never sought the job, but I'll do the best I can. All I want is to have a first-class police force." Although Horrall was chief for eight years, he spent this time mostly maintaining the status quo as the department waited out World War II.

However, he did have to deal with the "Zoot Suit Riots." Some pachucos—Mexican-American young men part of gangs—were known as zoot suiters for their distinctive baggy pants and oversized coats. In June 1943, several pachucos robbed a group of sailors on leave. The following day, scores of Navy men armed with makeshift weapons retaliated against the Hispanics living in East Los Angeles. As the LAPD moved to restore order, forty-four bruised and beaten zoot suiters were arrested for inciting a riot. The Navy men thought these arrests gave them the green light for further violence. Over the next four days, hundreds of citizens were injured in rioting. Seventeen youths were later convicted on various charges. Some community members felt sorry for the young men, whom they perceived as "naughty boys." The *LA Times* thought otherwise:

> The mush-headed sentimentalists are busy with their talk of "naughty boys" who should not be punished too severely. The fact that these young men wear silly looking zoot suits and that most of them are in their teens does not change the facts. It is hardly a boy's prank to invade peaceful social gatherings and knife people to death, or to pick up people off the street, drag them into automobiles, beat them and then throw them into the street bleeding and groaning.

While the LAPD was able to quell the Zoot Suit Riots, the department could not suppress its inner turmoil. Just ten years after the Shaw disgrace, another vice scandal had a devastating impact on the LAPD. A madam named Brenda Allen testified in a grand jury investigation involving the department, claiming she had the department's vice squad on her payroll. Chief Horrall and several officers were subsequently indicted for perjury. Mayor Bowron had enough and forced Horrall to retire. Although never convicted of wrongdoing, Horrall faded from the scene in 1949 after serving eight years as chief.

With Bowron leading the city, corruption in city hall was becoming just a bad memory. Vice was no longer making headlines and was becoming a non-issue. The LAPD was moving away from its dark past through Charter Section 202, better pay, and a robust pension system. The LAPD now had automatic pay increases and a promotion system based on merit, thus allowing ambitious and intelligent officers chances to lead. At the top, police managers took tests to get their positions, removing politics from deciding who gets the position.

The city financially supported training, which was critical to professionalizing the LAPD. The department now had elite instructors, such as William H. Parker and a University of Southern California professor. Applicants applied knowing they could become professional police officers who had job security. Los Angeles citizens were beginning to accept the idea of a proficient, accomplished police force no longer under the thumb of the criminal underworld and corrupt politicians.

With Chief Horrall forced out, the mayor was looking for someone new to lead the LAPD. The mayor needed an "emergency chief" until he could hold a search for someone new within the department. Without a convincing applicant from within, Mayor Bowron did as his predecessor had done in 1922 and turned to the military. On June 30, 1949, the mayor called on General William Worton (1949-1950), a decorated Marine who had just announced his retirement from the military.

After some arm twisting, Worton agreed to be the new LAPD chief. Upon taking command, he faced three distinct challenges: further professionalizing the department, eliminating leftover gangsters, and rooting out corruption. Worton was up for these challenges and took an entirely new and innovative approach.

In one of the LAPD's most defining moments, Chief Worton attacked the corruption problem from within the department. Worton developed the Internal Affairs Bureau to uncover and eliminate depravity and misconduct. Some of the best LAPD investigators were assigned to the new bureau. The "headhunters," as they were called, used trial boards and boards of inquiry to try accused officers. The bureau established an official method for handling complaints against officers. With no civilians to interfere with investigations, including the mayor, the department could boast about its strict internal trial system. Over the years, Internal Affairs became a conduit for promotion. Today, it (under different names) remains the lifeblood of the LAPD, ensuring there will be no return to the corrupt days.

To guarantee the Internal Affairs Bureau's success, as well as his own, Worton needed guidance—someone who knew the LAPD inside and out and someone he could trust. The name he heard repeated was William H. Parker. The inspector had over two decades of spotless service and the requisite Internal Affairs command credentials. Parker had held several managerial positions within the department, and as an executive officer for Chief James Davis, Parker had learned the intricacies of command. He was a graduate of the distinguished Northwestern University Traffic Management School. He taught at the police academy and the California Technical Institute of Police Officer Training. Parker had a law degree and was a member of the state bar. He also had wartime experience in formulating civilian police systems. And, with the backing of Chief Worton, Parker had the authority to openly pursue and root out any remaining corruption within the LAPD.

With Parker busy leading Internal Affairs, Chief Worton was the most effective outsider to lead the department until William Bratton took command five decades later. Using his military training and a distinct leadership command structure, Worton created a new LAPD organizational chart that delineated clear authority and responsibility for every major assignment. With this new structure, command officers knew exactly what was expected of them and the boundaries of their authority.

Worton also understood the need for an educated police officer, so he doubled the training period for recruits. He changed the standard of the way rookies began their careers. It had been common practice to assign new officers to Lincoln Heights Jail or have them direct traffic downtown—both assignments that dulled their enthusiasm as new police officers. Understanding this, Worton ended the practice and put these officers on patrol. Worton also merged the department's two gangster squads into a single intelligence squad and ordered these officers to work closely with the FBI on "antimob" activities. Finally, the new chief outlawed the ongoing practice of officers accepting gifts.

Worton used the ageless military motivation of spit and polish in conjunction with uncompromising inspections. A military man through and through, General Worton wanted the LAPD to share the same esprit de corps he had experienced in the Marine Corps—especially after morale was diminished following Chief Worton's forced retirement. Future Chief Edward M. Davis, who at the time was an impressionable young officer, recalled those days:

So they brought in a Marine general to straighten out the department. He was very gruff. I'll never forget him saying, "The only way to know if your department is good is to inspect, inspect and inspect—backwards, forwards and sideways."

Bob Rock, a future chief of the department, recalled:

[Worton] would be out prowling at night, and some guy would stop somebody to write a ticket. This big black car would pull up behind him, and when the officer was finished, this little guy would come walking over and say, "Hi, I'm the chief."

Chief Worton's military ethic appealed to the rank and file, particularly the LAPD's newest officers, many of whom were recently discharged following World War II. And the chief was just as proud of the department as the officers were of him. Worton preached:

You're cops, you're damned good ones. When you walk down the street, I want to see those chests out a mile, those heads carried high, and be damned proud when someone says, "There goes an LA cop."

In 1950, with his one-year tenure as emergency chief over, Worton stepped down—making room for a man who was destined for LAPD immortality.

The Liberator

Chief William H. Parker

"Now Parker, for his part of history, was the best thing for that police department that ever happened and the best thing for law enforcement that ever happened. Parker was a true professional."

—Thomas Reddin, Chief of Police

The Los Angeles Police Department has existed since 1851, when Dr. Alexander Hope was made its first chief. But in the subsequent 100 years, the department never functioned as well as it could have. Corruption and meddling politicians were the rule, not the exception. Parker changed all of that.

With Chief Worton ending his year of service, Mayor Bowron had interested command officers take the test to potentially become LAPD's next leader. Twenty-four command officers took the exam. When the results were announced in July 1950, William H. "Bill" Parker was at the top of the list, along with Thad Brown and Roger Murdock.

After meetings between the mayor and the police commission, they unanimously elected Parker.

On August 9, 1950, Bill Parker (1950-1966) became the chief of the LAPD. From then on, Parker would further professionalize the department and stomp out anyone who got in his way. The South Dakota native did away with the LAPD's habitual pattern of reform and corruption.

Anyone who worked for Bill Parker would tell you they would do anything for the man and the LAPD. He had a commanding presence and a no-nonsense way of getting things done. To street cops, he was known as an "iron ass," a strict disciplinarian who picked on officers and ran roughshod over people. But by the time Parker was finished, many officers had his photograph hanging in their homes because they loved the man and how he professionalized the department.

In his record-setting sixteen-year tenure as chief, Parker transformed the LAPD into an efficient, technologically advanced, and incorruptible operation—a model that other police departments worldwide would later emulate. No person in the LAPD's history has done more to professionalize the department than Parker. His protégé, the second longest-serving chief of police, Daryl F. Gates, said it best:

I am convinced that Chief Parker began LAPD. It existed before, but it didn't exist the way it existed after Parker became chief. He really was the heart and soul of that organization. He made it professional. He upgraded the quality of the people coming into that organization. He is the one who stamped honesty and integrity in the minds of every young recruit that came into the department. You just had that feeling you couldn't go bad because of LAPD and what it meant—and that's Bill Parker; that was his legacy. Just an incredible man and, in my judgment, probably the greatest chief LAPD ever had or will ever have.

Each generation of officers who have proudly pinned on the LAPD badge has left behind bits of their legacy for the future men and women of the Los Angeles Police Department to build upon. LAPD has grown stronger from those first six patrolmen to the over nine thousand highly trained professionals of today. Credit for this triumph belongs to the exceptional quality and dedication of the individual officer. Since the days of Bill Parker, the department has been committed to the impressive goal of maintaining an honest, corrupt-free police organization.

Not unlike the days of the Old West, the men and women who make up the LAPD see themselves as the "good guys"—and rightly so. They don't wear white hats, but they understand they are the difference between peace and chaos and will lay down their lives to protect the people of their beloved city. After all, they are Los Angeles police officers.

BIBLIOGRAPHY

Books Relating to the History of Los Angeles

Bell, Horace. *Reminiscences of a Ranger*. Los Angeles: Yarnell, Castile and Mathes, 1881.

———. *On The Old West Coast: Being Further Reminiscences of a Ranger*. New York: William Morrow & Co., 1902.

Bigger, Richard and James D. Kitchen. *How Cities Grew: A Century of Municipal Expansion*. In Metropolitan Los Angeles. Los Angeles: Haynes Foundation, 1952.

Bowman, Lynn. *Los Angeles: Epic of a City*. Berkeley, Calif: Howell-North Books, 1974.

Carr, Harry. Los Angeles: City of Dreams. New York: Frosset & Dunlap, 1935

Caughey, J., and L. Caughey, eds. *Los Angeles: Biography of a City*. Los Angeles: University of California Press, 1977.

Chronological Record of Los Angeles City Officials 1850-1930. Works Progress Administration, 1938.

Dyksta, Robert. Cattle Town. New York: Knopf, 1968.

Fogelson, Robert. *The Fragmented Metropolis: Los Angeles, 1850-1930*. Berkeley, Calif.: University of California Press, 1993.

Nadeau, Remi. *City Makers: The Story of Southern California's First Boom*. Corona del Mar, Calif.: Trans-Anglo Books, 1960.

———. Los Angeles: *From Mission to Modern City*. New York: Longman's Green & Co., 1960.

Newmark, Harris. *Sixty Years in Southern California, 1853-1913*. New York: The Knickerbocker Press, 1916.

Robinson, W.W. *Los Angeles From the Days of the Pueblo*. San Francisco: California Historical Society, 1959.

Willard, Dwight. *The History of Los Angeles City*. Los Angeles: Los Angeles Herald, 1901.

Wilson, Albert J. *History of Los Angeles County*, California. Oakland: Thompson and West, 1959.

Workman, Boyle. *The City that Grew*. Los Angeles: The Southland Publishing Co., 1935.

Zesch, Scott. *The Chinatown War: Chinese Los Angeles and the Massacre of 1871.* New York: Oxford University Press, 2012.

Articles, Newspapers, Documents, and Miscellaneous Relating to the History of the Los Angeles Police Department

Bultema, James. Unpublished script for a six-hour documentary, *Badge of Honor: An Insider's History of the Los Angeles Police Department.* 2002.

_____, ed. *The Link.* A publication of the Los Angeles Police Historical Society. Published quarterly 1993-2002.

Henstell, Bruce. "A Rogue's Gallery of Past Chiefs." *Los Angeles Magazine*, January 1978.

Los Angeles Police Department Annual Reports, 1891-2005.

Los Angeles Police Department. *The Beat*, 1947-1960.

Los Angeles Police Relief Association. *Annual Souvenir.* Frank C. Jenness, ed., 1911.

Los Angeles Police Revolver and Athletic Club. *The Guardian.* Published by the Los Angeles Police Department, 1937.

Interviews

All interviews listed below were conducted in the late 1990s and early 2000s by the author unless noted otherwise.

Chiefs of Police

Arthur C. Hohmann (oral interview in 1985)
Thomas Reddin
Edward M. Davis
Daryl F. Gates
Willie L. Williams
Bayan Lewis
Bernard Parks
Charlie Beck
Michel Moore

Authors

Joseph Wambaugh

Gerald Woods

Reporters

Pete Demetriou, radio
Jake Jacoby, a police beat reporter who worked out of Parker
    Center
Cecilia Rasmussen, *Los Angeles Times*

Los Angeles Police Department Officers, with their Retired Rank

Margaret Boyd, Policewoman
Rudy De Leon, Captain
Joe Dircks, Lieutenant
Mark Fuhrman, Detective
Gail Johnson, Policewoman
Richard Kalk, Detective
Betty Kelapez, Commander
Stacy Koon, Sergeant
Tom Lang, Detective
Ervis Lester, Deputy Chief
Greg Meyer, Captain
Roger Otis, Detective
John "Two Gun" Powers, Commander (Inspector)
Victor Reid, Policeman
Gordon Ring, Policeman
Art Sjoquist, Captain
Joseph Wambaugh, Detective
Roscoe "Rocky" Washington, Lieutenant (video interview by
    LAPD in 1987)
Dan Watson, Commander
Billy Wedgeworth, Commander
Richard Wemmer, Captain

Other Interviews

June Davis, daughter of Chief James E. Davis.
Mrs. Frank Harper, wife of Sergeant Frank Harper, first Medal
    of Valor winner.

Deforest Home, son of Chief George Home.

Phyllis Madone, widow of Patrolman Alfred Madone, an officer killed in the line of duty.

Bobbi Trout, reserve officer, the first female pilot of the LAPD.

Chapter 1: The Formative Years

Bell, Horace. *Reminiscences of a Ranger.* Los Angeles: Yarnell, Castile and Mathes, 1881.

———. *On the Old West Coast: Being Further Reminiscences of a Ranger.* New York: William Morrow & Co., 1902.

Blew, R.W. "Vigilantism in Los Angeles, 1835-1874." *Southern California Quarterly 44* (1972): 1, 11-30.

Boessenecker, J. Badge and Buckshot: *Lawlessness in Old California.* Oklahoma City: University of Oklahoma Press, 1988.

Fogelson, Robert. *The Fragmented Metropolis: Los Angeles, 1850-1930.* Los Angeles: University of California Press, 1993.

Los Angeles Common Council. "Resolution Memorializing the Death of Los Angeles City Marshal William C. Warren, November 5, 1870."

Los Angeles Daily News. "Los Angeles County Directory," March 10, 1869. Lists Warren as Marshal and Chief of Police.

Los Angeles Herald. "The Combination," (article deals with department politics), June 1, 1919.

Los Angeles Police Department Annual Report, 1889-1899.

Los Angeles Times. "Sebastian Made Police Chief; to Check Crime, His Promise," December 24, 1910.

———. "Our Police to Lead Country," July 29, 1912.

———. "Our War Squad is Commended," June 17, 1918.

Newmark, Harris. *Sixty Years in Southern California, 1853-1913.* New York: The Knickerbocker Press, 1916.Morrow & Co., 1902.

Chapter 2: The Fight for Control of LAPD

Los Angeles Herald. "The Federal Building," (in-depth article about city council members each fighting for their particular choice of chief—Chief Burns and nominee Glass), July 25, 1889.

———. "Another Row, The Police Commission Pot Again Boiling," September 20, 1889.

―――. No title (article about Chief John M. Glass calls him the best chief in the city's history), February 11, 1891.

―――. "The Police Victimized," March 31, 1892.

―――. "The Police Force," July 3, 1892.

―――. No title (deals with the politics of being chief), January 13, 1893.

―――. "The Counterfeiters," (article about detectives under Glass), June 26, 1894.

―――. "The War is Now On," (an in-depth article about the attempts to remove Chief Glass from office). November 19, 1896.

―――. "Proposed Salary Cut," October 29, 1897.

―――. "Tied Up too Long, Hitching Ordinance Violators Are Rounded Up by the Police," January 22, 1898.

―――. "A Covered Patrol Wagon," April 19, 1898.

―――. No title (deals with Chief Glass and the press), September 11, 1898.

―――. "Captain Bradish," (article about detectives and Bradish), September 14, 1898.

―――. "Annual Report," December 11, 1898.

―――. "Chief Glass Reprimanded," July 12, 1899.

―――. "Glass Asks to be Named Chief," (Glass attempted to get his old job back and was in the running up until the last minute), September 13, 1905.

Los Angeles Police Department Annual Report, 1897, Chief John M. Glass.

Los Angeles Times. "The Police Racket," December 27, 1899.

―――. "The Change Made: Chief Burns Gracefully Lays Down His Star," July 25, 1889.

San Francisco Call. "Bertillon System Prisoner's Undoing," May 13, 1909.

―――. "Los Angeles Reformers: Chief of Police Glass' Removal Demanded by the Ministerial Union," November 19, 1896.

―――. "Los Angeles Police Board, Police Commission vs. City Council," August 13, 1895.

Chapter 3: Civilian Chiefs of Police

Henstell, Bruce. Sunshine and Wealth: Los Angeles in the Twenties and Thirties. San Francisco: Chronicle Books, 1984.

Los Angeles Herald.

————. "Bedrock Shake-Up for Police Is Scheduled," (Chief Clarence Snively), September 11, 1916.

————. "Four Bids Received for Auto for Chief Dishman," November 3, 1909.

————. "Faithful Police Patrol Horses Are Worn Out By Killing Work," August 6, 1906.

————. "Patrolman Is A Real Hero," September 16, 1906.

————. "Plain Clothes Officers Make Numerous Arrests," July 28, 1908.

————. "Reports as to Uniforms for Special Officers," November 11,   1908.

————. "The Combination," (article deals with department politics), June 1, 1919.

————. "The Motorcycle Squad of the Los Angeles Police Department," November 21, 1909.

————. "Will Examine Workings of New Electric Patrol," November 24, 1909.

Los Angeles Police Department Annual Report. 1921, Chief Lyle Pendegast.

————. 1922, Chief Louis Oaks

Los Angeles Record, 1913-1926. Each issue has headlines and articles dealing with LAPD, corruption, politics, vice, and the chief of police.

Los Angeles Times. "Deputy Prosecutor is Made Chief of Police," October 31, 1920.

Chapter 4: Politics & The Battle Between Reform & Corruption

Annual Reports 1912-1916.

Daily Bulletin. Quote by Chief Sebastian. January 1911.

Los Angeles Times, miscellaneous dates.

————. "Sebastian Made police Chief: to Check Crime, His Promise," December 24, 1916.

Sebastian's business card with the quote, "Charles Sebastian, the People's Candidate for Mayor." Author's collection.

Chapter 5: Prohibition: Angels Awash in Alcohol

Bultema, James. "Back in Those Days," *The Link*, Volume 2, No. 2. July 1994.

Henstell, Bruce. *Sunshine and Wealth: Los Angeles in the Twenties and Thirties.* San Francisco: Chronicle Books, 1984.

Shawhan, Casey. "The Not So Angelic City," *Los Angeles Times.* August 31, 1980.

Chapter 6: Corruption Everywhere

Borough, Reuben W., "Law and Order in Los Angeles." *The Nation,* 125 (July 16, 1927).

Starr, Kevin. *Endangered Dreams: The Great Depression in California,* New York: Oxford University Press, 1996.

————. The Dream Endures: California Enters the 1940s. New York: Oxford University Press, 1997.

Chapter 7: The Revolving Door of Chiefs -
Vice & Corruption Take Their Toll

Henstell, Bruce. *Sunshine and Wealth: Los Angeles in the Twenties and Thirties.* San Francisco: Chronicle Books, 1984.

Los Angeles Times. "Deputy Prosecutor is Made Chief of Police," October 31, 1920.

Shawhan, Casey. "The Not So Angelic City," *Los Angeles Times,* August 31, 1980.

Chapter 8: The Man From Berkeley

Carte, Gene, and Elaine Carte. *Police Reform in the United States: The Era of August Vollmer.* Berkeley, Calif.: University of California Press, 1975.

Time magazine. "Finest of the Finest," February 18, 1966.

Parker, Alfred E. *Crime Fighter: August Vollmer.* New York: Macmillan Co., 1961.

Vollmer, August. *The Police and Modern Society. Berkeley, Calif.:* University of California Press, 1936.

Chapter 9: Gangsters, Prohibition, Corruption, and the
Nadir of LAPD

Bultema, James A. "Back in Those Days," *The Link*, Volume 2, No. 2. July 1994.

Heath, R. Lee. Correspondence to George Wilson, department historian, 3 pages. January 28, 1972.

———. Correspondence to George Wilson, 1 page, June 29, 1971.

———. Correspondence to George Wilson, 2 pages, April 17, 1972.

Los Angeles Herald. "Heath Rings in at End of Beat," no date.

Los Angeles Times.

———. "Civilians to Replace Officers in Clerical Jobs," August 8, 1924

———. "Dark Trails to City Hall are Uncovered: How Negro Politicians Make and Unmake Police Vice Squad Told in Heath Case," August 17, 1923.

———. "Heath After Vice Lords." July 31, 1924

———. "Kent Parrot Accused by Richards as 'Sinister.'" August 1, 1923.

———. "Oaks Names Kent Parrot, Charges Lawyer Interfered in Police Department, no date.

———. "Ousted Police Head Gives His Side of Row with Mayor," August 16, 1923.

———. "Police Pistol Range Opened," March 12, 1925.

———. "Police Class Graduates," September 21, 1924.

———. "Police Training School Standards Win Praise," April 18, 1926.

———. "These misguided gamblers are going to meet with bad luck," July 31, 1924.

———. "Thirty-three civilian employees to replace officers." August 29, 1924.

Sitton, Tom. *"The 'Boss' Without a Machine: Kent K. Parrot and Los Angeles Politics in the 1920s,"* Southern California Quarterly, Winter 1985.

Sjoquist, Arthur. "The Forgotten Chief," *The Link*, Volume 1, No. 1. Summer 1993.

Wilson, George D. "Chief R. Lee Heath," *The Beat,* January 1972.

Woods, Gerald J. *The Police in Los Angeles, Reform and Professionalization.* (Details that Heath disobeyed orders as told to the police commission.) New York: Garland Publishing, 1993.

Chapter 10: Gangster Versus Gangster: Fight for Control of the Liquor Business

Los Angeles Herald. "The Combination," (article deals with department politics), June 1, 1919.

———. "Bedrock Shake-Up for Police Is Scheduled," (Chief Clarence Snively), September 11, 1916.

Los Angeles Police Department Annual Reports, 1915-1930.

Los Angeles Police Department. Rules and Regulations for the Government of the Police Department, 1911.

Los Angeles Times. "Sebastian Made Police Chief; to Check Crime, His Promise," December 24, 1910.

———. "Our Police to Lead Country," July 29, 1912.

———. "Our War Squad is Commended," June 17, 1918.

Nathan, Albert. "How Whiskey Smugglers Buy and Land Cargoes, Well Organized Groups Engaged in Desperate Game of Rum-Running," *Los Angeles Times,* August 8, 1926.

Chapter 11: First Edition: Chief James E. Davis

Academy "Badge Day." Reconstruction of a typical "Badge Day" from this author's interviews with Lieutenant Joe Dircks and book by Domanick, Joe. *To Protect and to Serve: The LAPD's Century of War in the City of Dreams* pages 22-26.

Burton, Mary June. "The Runaway Boy Who Became Our Chief of Police," *Los Angeles Times,* September 24, 1933.

Dircks, J.O. Letter dated September 3, 1981, 3 pages. (Relates firsthand experience with the LAPD shooting team.)

Los Angeles Record. Breakfast Club. April 9, 1926.

Los Angeles Times.

———. Breakfast Club, March 20, 1926.

———. "Chief Davis Army Record.," "Chief Davis Early Days on Force." December 2, 1929.

———. "Chief Davis Tells of Gambling Raids. December 5, 1926.

———. "Chief Davis Tells of Gunfights." December 6, 1926.

———. "Chief Davis Talks About Vice Squad." December 4, 1926.

———. "How Chief Davis Became Chief." December 13, 1929.

———. "LA Police Chief Unravels Mystery of Private Cellar." November 30, 1929.

———. "Police Training School Wins Praise." April 8, 1926.

———. "'Rousting' System Earns Curses of the Rum-Runners, Chief Davis's Raids Keep Whiskey Ring in Harried State," *Los Angeles Times,* August 22, 1926.

———. "Vollmer Gives Davis Praise," October 15, 1929.

———. "What Kind of Person is Chief Davis." August 1, 1926.

Chapter 12: Gangsters Beware—There's a New Chief in Town

Borough, Reuben W. "Law and Order in Los Angeles." *The Nation*, 125 (July 16, 1927).

Los Angeles Record.

———. Davis after rum runners. August 5, 1926. Also, *Los Angeles Times,* August 25, 26, 1926. And, The *Guardians* publication of LAPD, 114-116.

———. "Mile Away Thomas Killed." August 19, 1929.

Los Angeles Times

———. Davis asks for 'Wheeled Forts.' May 19, 1926.

———. Thomas Shooting. April 22, 23, 1927.

Chapter 13: The Man with the Red Underwear

Los Angeles Record. Use of force quote. December 23, 1929.

Los Angeles Times. Quote supporting Chief Davis. August 2, 1928.

Mayor Porter supports Chief Davis. *Los Angeles Times,* October 19, 1929. And, "Mixing Fire, Brimstone and Politics," Cecilia Rasmussen, November 23, 1997, and Woods 125-128.

"New Day in the Police Commission," Police Commission Minutes, August 20, 1929.

Raid on House, Jacobson arrest. Domanick, 54-55, Woods, 114-115 and miscellaneous *Los Angeles Times* Articles, Cecilia Rasmussen, "Offices in Elite Team Did Things Their Way." August 8, 2004.

Support of Chief Davis, *Los Angeles Times Times*. November 12, 1929.

Vollmer supports Chief Davis. *Los Angeles Times*. October 15, 1929.

Chapter 14: Fight for Control of the City

Los Angeles Times
————. "Kent Parrot Accused by Richards as 'Sinister.'" August 1, 1923.
————. "Oaks Names Kent Parrot, Charges Lawyer Interfered in Police Department, 'Dictatorial and Threatening,'" July 29, 1923.
————."Ousted Police Head Gives His Side of Row with Mayor," August 16, 1923.
————. Shooting of Crawford. *Los Angeles Times*, no date.
The Great Los Angeles Swindle, 306-308. Woods, 147.
Sitton, Tom. "The 'Boss' Without a Machine: Kent K. Parrot and Los Angeles Politics in the 1920s," *Southern California Quarterly,* Winter 1985.
Wilson, George D. "Chief R. Lee Heath," *The Beat*, January 1972.
Woods, Gerald J. The Police in Los Angeles, Reform and Professionalization. (Details that Heath disobeyed orders as told to the police commission.) New York: Garland Publishing, 1993.

Chapter 15: Second Edition: The Return of James E. Davis and

Chapter 16: Righting a Wrong – Davis Leads Fight for Political Independence

Davis, James E., chief of police. "Why Police Women?" *Los Angeles Times,* no date.

———. "Careers in the Public Service of Los Angeles." *The Los Angeles City Employee.* April 1936

Los Angeles Times. "J.E. Davis, Retired Police Chief, Dies," June 21, 1949.

———. "Chief Davis Orders Complete 'Cleanup' of L.A. Vice Spots," July 13, 1937.

———. "Chief of Police Davis." August 11, 1933.

———. "Chief Tells Crime Drop," February 13, 1936.

———. "Chief Davis to Carry War to Criminal." August 27, 1933. And Woods, 142.

———. "Davis Slated As Police Chief." August 9, 1933.

———. "Death Urged For Bandits," May 26, 1934.

———. "Davis Fetes Marksman," July 24, 1935. (Mexican pistol team guest at the academy.)

———. "Ex-Chief Davis Says Good-Bye," November 19, 1938.

———. "L.A. Vice Probe Demanded," no date.

———. Opening quote, June 5, 2020

———. "The Chief of Police," November 18, 1938.

———. "Thirty-Five Men In Room Guide Police Radio Cars." September 21, 1936.

———. "War On Gangsters Starts," August 30, 1933.

Chapter 17: The "West Point" of Police Academies

Chief Davis is given credit for Police Academy. *Los Angeles Times,* August 23, 1936, and April 26, 1939.

Los Angeles Times. "Dark Trails to City Hall are Uncovered: How Negro Politicians Make and Unmake Police Vice Squad Told in Heath Case," August 17, 1923.

———. "Police Build 'West Point,'" March 27, 1938.

———. "Police Class Graduates," September 21, 1924.

———. "Police Pistol Range Opened," March 12, 1925.

———. "Police Training School Standards Win Praise," April
     18, 1926.
The Link. "Birth of the Los Angeles Police Academy," Volume
     1, No. 2. Late fall 1993.

Chapter 18: The Bum Blockades
Chief Davis and Constitutional Rights. *Los Angeles Record*
December 23, 1929. And, *Los Angeles Times*, February 10,
1936.
     Chief Davis' speech to church. Los Angles *Times,* February
10, 1936.
     Chief Davis receives accolades for the blockade. Los Angeles
Times, February 27, 1936.
     Los Angeles Examiner. "Plan Blockade on Transients," no
date.
     Los Angeles Police Department. Official report No. 72 on the
blockade in Imperial County on U.S. Highway 80 and S.P.
Railway. Sergeant D.A. McCoole. February 11, 1936. These
reports list the number of suspects encountered and give
statistics and a general overview of the officers' activities.
———. Sergeant Cole. February 29, 1936. Letter to Captain
     Horrall reporting the arrest of a suspect for burglary.
———. Sergeant Don Douglas. February 7, 1936.
———. Form 171, arrest report of murder suspect. February 5,
1936.
     Mayor orders Blockade, *Los Angeles Times Times* February 6,
1936.
     Wild, Mark. "LA Police Declares War on 47 States."
California Historical Society, no date.
     Private correspondence from an unknown officer to Captain
C.B. Horrall from Needles, California. (Discusses activity on
transients coming into the state.) Two pages. February 7, 1936

Chapter 19: The Red Squad
Bloom, Hannah. "The Passing of Red Hynes." *The Nation*,
175 (August 2, 1952): 91-92.

Fight in the chambers of the City Council. *Los Angeles Times*, February 16, 1933.

Hynes was assigned to WLA Division. *Los Angeles Times Times* December 1, 1938

Chapter 20: The Battle for Control of the County Grand Jury

Gangsters brag about owning the grand jury. Woods 171.

Judge Bowron forms a grand jury. *Los Angeles Times Times*, February 16, 1934.

Corrupt city officials. *Los Angeles Times Times* November 14, 21, 27, 1934.

Chapter 21: The Explosive End to Corruption

Los Angeles Times. "Penny Money At Café: Clinton 'Cafeteria' Caters to Customers of Lean Purse," October 14, 1932.

———. "Davis Clears Kynette and Squad in Harry Raymond Bombing," January 24, 1938.

———. "Bullets Pierce Chief's Window," March 31, 1938.

———. "Testimony of Kynette at Bomb Trial," May 25, 1938.

———. "Chief Davis Asks Retirement; Will Remain if Bowron Wishes," November 17, 1938.

———. "Bowron Calls on Police Board to Replace Chief Davis at Once," November 18, 1938.

———. "Davis Defends Police Spying at Bombing Trial, Bitter Clashes Mark Chief's Day on Stand," April 27, 1939.

———. "Police Due for Shake-up Tomorrow, Chief Announces: New Divisions Will Be Organized and Shifts Made of Many Uniformed   Officers in Sweeping Program," November 30, 1939.

Police and crime sections of the speakers manual and campaign textbook for Mayor Bowron. Compiled by the Citizens Committee to Re-Elect Mayor Bowron. UCLA Research Library-Special Collections,
Clifford Clinton Collection, 1941.

Porter, John C., mayor. "Is Los Angeles Wicked? Is Vice Still Rampant?" *Los Angeles Times*, June 29, 1933.

Shooting of Bruneman. *Los Angeles Times Times*. October 26, 1937.

Viche, Fred W. "The Recall of Mayor Frank L. Shaw, Revision," 12-page article, no date.

Chapter 22: New Beginnings – The Shields

Badges. *Los Angeles Times Times*. October 28, 1938.

Bultema, James "Chiefs' Corner: A Talk with the Past," *The Link,* Volume 1, No. 2. Late fall 1993.

———. "Chiefs' Corner: A Talk with the Past," The *Link,* Volume 2, No. 1. April 1994.

———. Interview with retired Chief Arthur Hohmann, 1985.

Chicago Sun-Times. "Ex-Marine Tightened Up Los Angeles Police," March 12, 1952.

James, Thomas H. *"Chief Steckel Unmasked,"* (68-page expose on corruption on the LAPD and city government). Written by six-year veteran of LAPD who was fired. 1931.

Johnson, Gail F. "A Tribute to Chief Parker," *The Link*, Volume 3, No. 1. June 1996

The Los Angeles City Employee. "Los Angeles Police Force Upholds Proud Traditions." April 1936

Los Angeles Times. "Chief Shifts 28 Officers In New Shake-Up of Police," March 8, 1939.

———. "Davis Discloses 7843 Civilians Given Badges," October 27, 1938.

———. "Hohmann Made Chief; Takes New Post Today," June 24, 1939.

———. "New Type of Police Badges Offered for Board's Approval," August 9, 1939.

Page, Jim. "Deputy Chief Arthur C. Hohmann Retires," *Los Angeles Police Beat,* no date.

———. "Police Badge Holders List Checked by Mayor," October 28, 1938. (Provides a very detailed list of those who received police badges.)

————. "Policewoman Implicates Sgt. Stoker in Burglary, Love for Vice Squad Man Admitted by Audrey [sic] Davis," July 3, 1949.

Stoker, Charles. *Thicker 'N Thieves: The 1950 Factual Expose of Police Pay-Offs, Graft, Political Corruption and Prostitution in Los Angeles and Hollywood.* Santa Monica, Calif.: Sidereal Co. 1951.

Turner, Timothy G. "Significance of Zoot-Suit Gangsters," *Los Angeles Times,* January 14, 1943.

————. "Zoot Suit War Runs Course as Riots Subside," June 12, 1943.

Chapter 23: The Liberator: Chief William H. Parker

Jennings, Dean. "Portrait of a Police Chief," Saturday Evening Post, May 7, 1960.

Los Angeles Police Beat. "Biography of William H. Parker," entire issue. September 1966.

Los Angeles Times. "LAPD Chief Parker: a product of his time," January 28, 2009.

————. "The Bright Badge of the LAPD," August 9, 1960.

————. "Chief Parker Molded LAPD Image-Then Came the '60s. Police," May 25, 1992.

Martin, Glynn B. "LAPD Chief Parker: A product of his time." *Los Angeles Times,* January 28, 2009.

Marx, Wesley. "Parker: The Cop as Crusader." *Los Angeles Magazine*, August 1962.

U.S. News & World Report. "A Police Chief Talks of Police Brutality," August 10, 1964.

Webb, Jack. *The Badge.* Englewood Cliffs, N.J.:Prentice-Hall, 1958.

Weeks, Paul. "Story of Chief Parker, Enemy of the Criminal." *Los Angeles Mirror*, June 17, 1957.

CPSIA information can be obtained
at www.ICGtesting.com
Printed in the USA
JSHW010052130523
41669JS00008B/426